Second Workshop on Statistical Parsing of Morphologically Rich Languages 2011

(SPMRL 2011)

Co-located with IWPT 2011

Dublin, Ireland
6 October 2011

ISBN: 978-1-61839-256-5

Printed from e-media with permission by:

Curran Associates, Inc.
57 Morehouse Lane
Red Hook, NY 12571

Some format issues inherent in the e-media version may also appear in this print version.

Printed by Curran Associates, Inc. (2011)

Association for Computational Linguistics
209 N. Eighth Street
Stroudsburg, Pennsylvania 18360

Phone: 1-570-476-8006
Fax: 1-570-476-0860

acl@aclweb.org

Additional copies of this publication are available from:

Curran Associates, Inc.
57 Morehouse Lane
Red Hook, NY 12571 USA
Phone: 845-758-0400
Fax: 845-758-2634
Email: curran@proceedings.com
Web: www.proceedings.com

Forewords

Welcome to the second workshop on Statistical Parsing of Morphologically Rich Languages! Following the warm reception of the first official SPMRL workshop at NAACL-HLT 2010, our aim with the second workshop is to build upon the success of the first and offer a platform to the growing community of people who are interested in developing tools and resources for parsing MRLs. We decided to collocate with the International Workshop on Parsing Technologies (IWPT), both because the themes of the two events are so closely related and because the seeds of the SPMRL workshop were planted during IWPT 2009 in Paris. The warm welcome and support of the IWPT community made it our unequivocal choice, and we are honored and pleased to collocate our second SPMRL workshop with this year's IWPT event

Fourteen papers were submitted in total to the workshop. After two withdrawals,we chose to accept four long papers and four short papers, giving an acceptance rate of 66%. Our goal during the selection process was to produce a varied, balanced and interesting program without compromising on quality, and we believe that we have achieved this goal. This year's papers cover a broad range of languages (Arabic, Basque, French, German, Hindi, Korean,Turkish) and are concerned with the most pressing issues (handling discontinuity, incorporating morphological information, the problems of real-world text) over a range of parsing approaches (discriminative and generative, constituency and dependency) We believe that they will result in a lively and productive workshop.

We are continuing the SPMRL tradition of ending the workshop with a panel discussion. We are very proud of this year's panel and are very grateful to our panellists (Josef van Genabith , James Henderson, Joakim Nivre, Slav Petrov and Yannick Versley) for agreeing to participate. This year's main theme for the panel will be the design of a shared task on parsing MRLs, in the face of various challenges that emerge when going beyond English and the WSJ Penn Treebank. A typical challenge when moving away from parsing English to other languages, is, for instance, the nature of the input, which consists of unanalyzed non-gold word tokens. Additional challenges have to do with the typological diversity of the syntactic structures and sound evaluation across experiments using different corpora. Our ultimate goal in this panel will be to tease apart the various issues we need to address and understand how we might organize a shared task that will bring our burgeoning field forward.

Finally, we would like to express our gratitude to the following people who helped us organise SPMRL 2011: the IWPT chairs, Joakim Nivre and his limitless availibility, Özlem Çetinoğlu and Harry Bunt, Alon Lavie and Kenji Sagae from SIGPARSE who continue to support this workshop, Josef van Genabith, Laurence Danlos and, last but not least, our very knowledgeable and hard-working review committee who did a sterling job during the off-peak review season. Thanks guys!

The SPMRL 2011 Program Committee

Program Chairs:

Djamé Seddah, INRIA/University of Paris-Sorbonne (France)
Reut Tsarfaty, Uppsala University (Sweden)
Jennifer Foster, NCLT, Dublin City University (Ireland)

Program Committee:

Marie Candito, INRIA/University Paris 7 (France)
Yoav Goldberg, Ben Gurion University of the Negev (Israel)
Ines Rehbein, Universität Saarbrücken (Germany)
Lamia Tounsi, NCLT, Dublin City University (Ireland)
Yannick Versley, Universität Tübingen (Germany)

Review Committee:

Mohammed Attia (Dublin City University, Ireland)
Bernd Bohnet (University of Stuttgart, Germany)
Adriane Boyd (Ohio State University, USA)
Özlem Çetinoğlu (Dublin City University, Ireland)
Grzegorz Chrupała (Saarland University, Germany)
Benoit Crabbé (University of Paris 7, France)
Josef van Genabith (Dublin City University, Ireland)
Spence Green (Stanford University, US)
Deirdre Hogan (Dublin City University, Ireland)
Samar Husain (Inter. Institute of Information Technology, India)
Sandra Kuebler (Indiana University, US)
Jonas Kuhn (University of Stuttgart, Germany)
Alberto Lavelli (FBK-irst, Italy)
Joseph Le Roux (Dublin City University, Ireland)
Wolfgang Maier (University of Tüebingen, Germany)
Yuval Marton (IBM Watson Resarch Center, US)
Takuya Matsuzaki (University of Toyko, Japan)
Yusuke Miyao (University of Toyko, Japan)
Joakim Nivre (Uppsala University, Sweden)
Ines Rehbein (Saarland University, Germany)
Owen Rambow (Columbia University, US)
Kenji Sagae (University of Southern California, USA)
Benoit Sagot (Inria Rocquencourt, France)

Panelists:

Josef van Genabith (Dublin City University, Ireland)
James Henderson (Université de Geneve, Switzerland)
Joakim Nivre (Uppsala University, Sweden)
Slav Petrov (Google Research NY, USA)
Reut Tsarfaty (Chair, Uppsala University, Sweden)
Yannick Versley (University of Tübingen, Germany)

Table of Contents

Workshop Program

Thursday October 6, 2011

13:30–13:35 **Opening Remarks**

13:35-14:45 **Session 1** (Chair: Djamé Seddah)

Statistical Dependency Parsing in Korean: From Corpus Generation To Automatic Parsing
Jinho D. Choi and Martha Palmer

Morphological Features for Parsing Morphologically-rich Languages: A Case of Arabic
Jon Dehdari, Lamia Tounsi and Josef van Genabith

French parsing enhanced with a word clustering method based on a syntactic lexicon
Anthony Sigogne, Matthieu Constant and Eric Laporte

Testing the Effect of Morphological Disambiguation in Dependency Parsing of Basque
Kepa Bengoetxea, Arantza Casillas and Koldo Gojenola

14:45–15:05 **Break**

15:05-16:15 **Session 2** (Chair: Jennifer Foster)

Discontinuous Data-Oriented Parsing: A mildly context-sensitive all-fragments grammar
Andreas van Cranenburgh, Remko Scha and Federico Sangati

Multiword Expressions in Statistical Dependency Parsing
Gulsen Erygit, Tugay Ilbay and Ozan Arkan Can

Linguistically Rich Graph Based Data Driven Parsing For Hindi
Samar Husain, Raghu Pujitha Gade and Rajeev Sangal

Data point selection for self-training
Ines Rehbein

Thursday October 6, 2011 (continued)

16:15-16:25 **Short Break**

16:25-17:25 **Discussion Panel: Josef van Genabith, James Hendersen, Joakim Nivre, Slav Petrov, Yannick Versley** (Chair: Reut Tsarfaty)

17:25-17:30 **Concluding Remarks**

Statistical Dependency Parsing in Korean: From Corpus Generation To Automatic Parsing

Jinho D. Choi
Department of Computer Science
University of Colorado at Boulder
choijd@colorado.edu

Martha Palmer
Department of Linguistics
University of Colorado at Boulder
mpalmer@colorado.edu

Abstract

This paper gives two contributions to dependency parsing in Korean. First, we build a Korean dependency Treebank from an existing constituent Treebank. For a morphologically rich language like Korean, dependency parsing shows some advantages over constituent parsing. Since there is not much training data available, we automatically generate dependency trees by applying head-percolation rules and heuristics to the constituent trees. Second, we show how to extract useful features for dependency parsing from rich morphology in Korean. Once we build the dependency Treebank, any statistical parsing approach can be applied. The challenging part is how to extract features from tokens consisting of multiple morphemes. We suggest a way of selecting important morphemes and use only these as features to avoid sparsity. Our parsing approach is evaluated on three different genres using both gold-standard and automatic morphological analysis. We also test the impact of fine vs. coarse-grained morphologies on dependency parsing. With automatic morphological analysis, we achieve labeled attachment scores of $80\%^{+}$. To the best of our knowledge, this is the first time that Korean dependency parsing has been evaluated on labeled edges with such a large variety of data.

1 Introduction

Statistical parsing has recently been popular in the NLP community; most state-of-the-art parsers take various statistical approaches to achieve their performance (Johnson and Ural, 2010; Nivre and McDonald, 2008). The biggest advantage of statistical parsing over rule-based parsing is that it can automatically adapt to new domains, genres, or languages as long as it is provided with enough and proper training data. On the other hand, this can also be the biggest drawback for statistical parsing because annotating such training data is manually intensive work that may be costly and time consuming.

For a morphologically rich language like Korean, dependency parsing shows some advantages over constituent parsing. Unlike phrase structure that is somewhat restricted by word-order (e.g., an object needs to be followed by a verb), dependency structure does not enforce such restrictions (e.g., an object is a dependent of a verb in any position), which makes it more suitable for representing flexible word-order languages. Korean is known to be a flexible word-order language in that although it generally follows the SOV (subject-object-verb) construction, it still accepts sentences following different orders. This is because subjects and objects are usually attached to case particles, so locating them in different positions does not create too much ambiguity. Furthermore, these morphemes (case particles along with many others) often give important clues about dependency relations to their heads, which become very helpful for dependency parsing.

To perform statistical dependency parsing, we need sufficiently large training data. There is not much training data available for dependency structure in Korean. However, there is a Treebank, called the Sejong Treebank[1], containing a large number of constituent trees in Korean (about 60K sentences),

[1] http://www.sejong.or.kr/eindex.php

formated similarly to the Penn Treebank (Marcus et al., 1993). The Penn Treebank style constituent trees have been reliably converted to dependency trees using head-percolation rules and heuristics (Marneffe et al., 2006; Johansson and Nugues, 2007). By applying a similar conversion strategy to the Sejong Treebank, we can achieve a large set of training data for Korean dependency parsing.

Once we generate the dependency Treebank, any statistical dependency parsing approach can be applied (McDonald et al., 2005; Nivre, 2008). The challenging part is how to extract features from tokens consisting of multiple morphemes. For example, POS tags are typical features for dependency parsing under an assumption that each token consists of a single POS tag. This assumption is only partially true in Korean; a token can consist of a sequence of morphemes with different POS tags.[2]

말한다	➔	말/NNG	한/XSV	다/EF
talk (verb)		talk (noun)	do	ending_marker

Figure 1: Morphological analysis of a verb *talk* in Korean. POS tags are described in Table 1.

In Figure 1, a verb *talk* in Korean consists of three morphemes, *talk* as a noun, *do* as a verb-derivational suffix, and a final ending marker, such that although it appears to be a single token, it is really a sequence of three individual morphemes where each morpheme has its own POS tag. It is not clear which combination of these morphemes yields the best representation of the token for dependency parsing. Moreover, deriving joined features from multiple tokens (e.g., a joined feature of POS tags between two tokens) can be problematic; considering all combinations of morphemes within multiple tokens can be cumbersome and generate very sparse features.

Obviously, having a good morphological analysis is very important for parsing. There are many automatic morphological analyzers available in Korean (Kang and Woo, 2001; Shim and Yang, 2002). Some of them use different kinds of morphologies better suited for their purposes. It is useful to have a fine-grained morphology; however, a more fine-grained morphology does not necessarily mean a better morphology for parsing. For instance, breaking a token into too many morphemes may cause a loss in the overall semantics of the token. Thus, it is worth comparing outputs from different morphological analyzers and seeing how much impact each morphology has on dependency parsing.

In this paper, we present head-percolation rules and heuristics to convert constituent trees in the Sejong Treebank to dependency trees. We then suggest a way of selecting important morphemes for dependency parsing. To get automatically generated morphemes, we use two existing morphological analyzers. All parsing models are built by a transition-based parsing algorithm. We evaluate our models on test sets in three different genres. Each test set is evaluated by using both gold-standard and automatic morphological analysis. We also compare the impact of fine-grained vs. coarse-grained morphologies on dependency parsing. To the best of our knowledge, this is the first time that Korean dependency parsing has been evaluated on labeled edges with such a large variety of data.

2 Related work

Marneffe et al. (2006) introduced a system for extracting typed dependencies from the Penn Treebank style constituent trees, known as the Stanford dependencies. Johansson and Nugues (2007) presented the LTH constituent-to-dependency converter that had been used to prepare English data for the CoNLL'08-09 shared tasks (Surdeanu et al., 2008; Hajič et al., 2009). Choi and Palmer (2010) later enhanced Johansson and Nugues' approach to handle new updates in the latest Penn Treebank format.

Besides the Sejong Treebank, there are few other Korean Treebanks available. The Penn Korean Treebank (Han et al., 2002) contains the Penn Treebank style constituent trees for newswire and military corpora (about 15K sentences combined). There is also the KAIST tree-annotated corpus (Lee, 1998) containing constituent trees annotated by different bracketing guidelines from the Penn Korean Treebank (about 30K sentences). We chose the Sejong Treebank because it is the largest and most recent Korean Treebank including several function tags that are useful for the dependency conversion.

[2]English words can consist of multiple morphemes as well (e.g., buying → buy/verb + ing/progressive_suffix), but such morphology is usually not used in parsing.

NNG	General noun	MM	Adnoun	EP	Prefinal EM	JX	Auxiliary PR
NNP	Proper noun	MAG	General adverb	EF	Final EM	JC	Conjunctive PR
NNB	Bound noun	MAJ	Conjunctive adverb	EC	Conjunctive EM	IC	Interjection
NP	Pronoun	JKS	Subjective CP	ETN	Nominalizing EM	SN	Number
NR	Numeral	JKC	Complemental CP	ETM	Adnominalizing EM	SL	Foreign word
VV	Verb	JKG	Adnomial CP	XPN	Noun prefix	SH	Chinese word
VA	Adjective	JKO	Objective CP	XSN	Noun DS	NF	Noun-like word
VX	Auxiliary predicate	JKB	Adverbial CP	XSV	Verb DS	NV	Predicate-like word
VCP	Copula	JKV	Vocative CP	XSA	Adjective DS	NA	Unknown word
VCN	Negation adjective	JKQ	Quotative CP	XR	Base morpheme	SF, SP, SS, SE, SO, SW	

Table 1: POS tags in the Sejong Treebank (PM: predicate marker, CP: case particle, EM: ending marker, DS: derivational suffix, PR: particle, SF SP SS SE SO: different types of punctuation).

Automatic morphological analysis has been one of the most broadly explored topics in Korean NLP. Kang and Woo (2001) presented the KLT morphological analyzer, which has been widely used in Korea. The Sejong project distributed the Intelligent Morphological Analyzer (IMA), used to pre-process raw texts in the Sejong Treebank.[3] Shim and Yang (2002) introduced another morphological analyzer, called Mach, optimized for speed; it takes about 1 second to analyze 1.3M words yet performs very accurately. Han (2005) presented a finite-state transducer that had been used to check morphology in the Penn Korean Treebank. We use IMA and Mach to generate fine-grained (IMA) and coarse-grained (Mach) morphologies for our experiments.

Statistical dependency parsing has been explored relatively little in Korean. Chung (2004) presented a dependency parsing model using surface contextual information. This parser can be viewed as a probabilistic rule-based system that gathers probabilities from features like lexical items, POS tags, and distances. Oh and Cha (2008) presented another statistical dependency parsing model using cascaded chunking for parsing and conditional random fields for learning. Our work is distinguished from theirs in mainly two ways. First, we add labels to dependency edges during the conversion, so parsing performance can be evaluated on both labels and edges. Second, we selectively choose morphemes useful for dependency parsing, which prevents generating very sparse features. The morpheme selection is done automatically by applying our linguistically motivated rules (cf. Section 5.3).

[3]The system is not publicly available but can be requested from the Sejong project (http://www.sejong.or.kr).

Han et al. (2000) presented an approach for handling structural divergence and recovering dropped arguments in a Korean-to-English machine translation system. In their approach, they used a Korean dependency parser for lexico-structural processing.

3 Constituent-to-dependency conversion

3.1 Constituent trees in the Sejong Treebank

The Sejong Treebank contains constituent trees similar to ones in the Penn Treebank.[4] Figure 2 shows a constituent tree and morphological analysis for a sentence, *She still loved him*, in Korean.

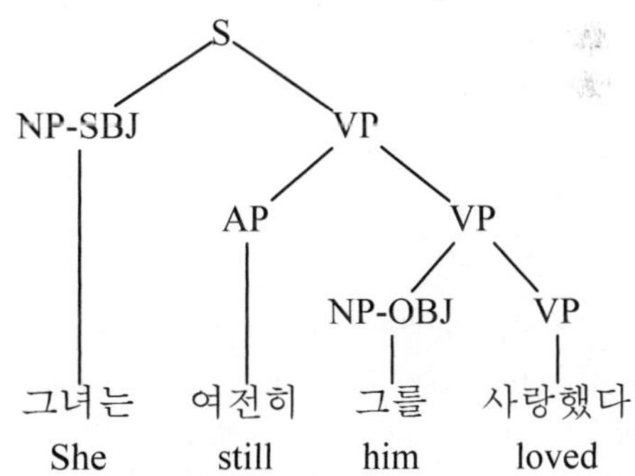

그녀는 → 그녀(she)/NP+는/JX

여전히 → 여전히(still)/MAG

그를 → 그(he)/NP+를/JKO

사랑했다 → 사랑(love)/NNG+하/XSV+았/EP+다/EF

Figure 2: A constituent tree and morphological analysis for a sentence, *She still loved him*, in Korean.

[4]The bracketing guidelines can be requested from the Sejong project, available only in Korean.

The tree consists of phrasal nodes as described in Table 2. Each token can be broken into several morphemes annotated with POS tags (Table 1). In the Sejong Treebank, tokens are separated mostly by white spaces; for instance, an item like 'A(B+C)D' is considered as a single token because it does not contain any white space in between. As a result, a token can be broken into as many as 21 individual morphemes (e.g., 'A', '(', 'B', '+', 'C', ')', 'D').

Notice that some phrases are annotated with function tags (Table 2). These function tags show dependency relations between the tagged phrases and their siblings, so can be used as dependency labels during the conversion. There are three other special types of phrase-level tags besides the ones in Table 2. X indicates phrases containing only case particles, ending markers, or punctuation. L and R indicate phrases containing only left and right brackets, respectively. These tags are also used to determine dependency relations during the conversion.

Phrase-level tags		Function tags	
S	Sentence	SBJ	Subject
Q	Quotative clause	OBJ	Object
NP	Noun phrase	CMP	Complement
VP	Verb phrase	MOD	Noun modifier
VNP	Copula phrase	AJT	Predicate modifier
AP	Adverb phrase	CNJ	Conjunctive
DP	Adnoun phrase	INT	Vocative
IP	Interjection phrase	PRN	Parenthetical

Table 2: Phrase-level tags (left) and function tags (right) in the Sejong Treebank.

3.2 Head-percolation rules

Table 3 gives the list of head-percolation rules (from now on, headrules), derived from analysis of each phrase type in the Sejong Treebank. Except for the quotative clause (Q), all other phrase types try to find their heads from the rightmost children, which aligns with the general concept of Korean being a head-final language. Note that these headrules do not involve the POS tags in Table 1; those POS tags are used only for morphemes within tokens (and each token is annotated with a phrase-level tag). It is possible to extend the headrules to token-level and find the head morpheme of each token; however, finding dependencies between different morphemes within a token is not especially interesting although there are some approaches that have treated each morpheme as an individual token to parse (Chung et al., 2010).[5]

S	r	VP;VNP;S;NP|AP;Q;*
Q	l	S|VP|VNP|NP;Q;*
NP	r	NP;S;VP;VNP;AP;*
VP	r	VP;VNP;NP;S;IP;*
VNP	r	VNP;NP;S;*
AP	r	AP;VP;NP;S;*
DP	r	DP;VP;*
IP	r	IP;VNP;*
X|L|R	r	*

Table 3: Head-percolation rules for the Sejong Treebank. l/r implies looking for the leftmost/rightmost constituent. * implies any phrase-level tag. | implies a logical OR and ; is a delimiter between tags. Each rule gives higher precedence to the left (e.g., S takes the highest precedence in VP).

Once we have the headrules, it is pretty easy to generate dependency trees from constituent trees. For each phrase (or clause) in a constituent tree, we find the head of the phrase using its headrules and make all other nodes in the phrase dependents of the head. The procedure goes on recursively until every node in the tree finds its head (for more details, see Choi and Palmer (2010)). A dependency tree generated by this procedure is guaranteed to be well-formed (unique root, single head, connected, and acyclic); however, it does not include labels yet. Section 3.3 shows how to add dependency labels to these trees. In addition, Section 3.4 describes heuristics to resolve some of the special cases (e.g., coordinations, nested function tags).

It is worth mentioning that constituent trees in the Sejong Treebank do not include any empty categories. This implies that dependency trees generated by these headrules consist of only projective dependencies (non-crossing edges; Nivre and Nilsson (2005)). On the other hand, the Penn Korean Treebank contains empty categories representing long-distance dependencies. It will be interesting to see if we can train empty category insertion and resolution models on the Penn Korean Treebank, run the mod-

[5]Chung et al. (2010) also showed that recovering certain kinds of null elements improves PCFG parsing, which can be applied to dependency parsing as well.

els on the Sejong Treebank, and use the automatically inserted and linked empty categories to generate non-projective dependencies.

3.3 Dependency labels

Two types of dependency labels are derived from the constituent trees. The first type includes labels retained from the function tags. When any node annotated with a function tag is determined to be a dependent of some other node by our headrules, the function tag is taken as the dependency label to its head. Figure 3 shows a dependency tree converted from the constituent tree in Figure 2, using the function tags as dependency labels (SBJ and OBJ).

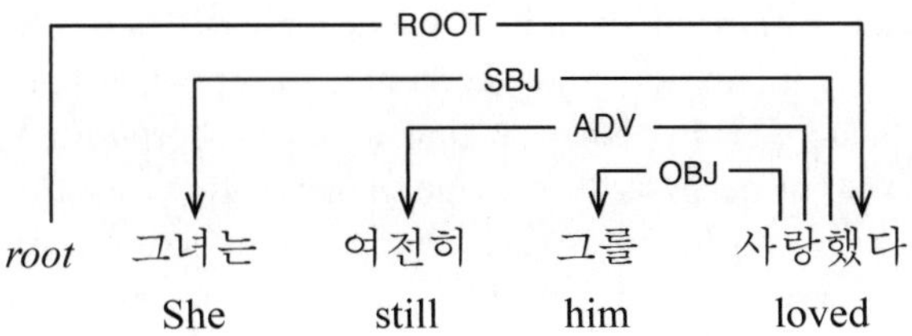

Figure 3: A dependency tree with labels, converted from the constituent tree in Figure 2.

The other labels (ROOT and ADV) belong to the second type; these are labels inferred from constituent relations. Algorithm 1 shows how to infer these labels given constituents c and p, where c is a dependent of p according to our headrules. ROOT is the dependency label of the root node (*root* in Figure 3). ADV is for adverbials, and (A | D | N | V) MOD are for (adverb, adnoun, noun, verb) modifiers, respectively. DEP is the default label used when no condition is met. These inferred labels are used when c is not annotated with a function tag.

There are two other special types of labels. A dependency label P is assigned to all punctuation regardless of function tags or constituent relations. Furthermore, when c is a phrase type X, a label X is conjoined with its genetic dependency label (e.g., CMP $\rightarrow$ X_CMP). This is because the phrase type X usually consists of morphemes detached from their head phrases (e.g., case particles, ending markers), so should have distinguished dependency relations from other standalone tokens. Table 4 shows the distribution of all labels in the Sejong Treebank (in percentile).

input : (c, p), where c is a dependent of p.
output: A dependency label l as $c \xleftarrow{l} p$.
begin
  if $p = root$ **then** ROOT $\rightarrow l$
  elif c.pos = AP **then** ADV $\rightarrow l$
  elif p.pos = AP **then** AMOD $\rightarrow l$
  elif p.pos = DP **then** DMOD $\rightarrow l$
  elif p.pos = NP **then** NMOD $\rightarrow l$
  elif p.pos = VP | VNP | IP **then** VMOD $\rightarrow l$
  else DEP $\rightarrow l$
end

Algorithm 1: Getting inferred labels.

AJT	11.70	MOD	18.71	X	0.01
CMP	1.49	AMOD	0.13	X_AJT	0.08
CNJ	2.47	DMOD	0.02	X_CMP	0.11
INT	0.09	NMOD	13.10	X_CNJ	0.02
OBJ	8.95	VMOD	20.26	X_MOD	0.07
PRN	0.15	ROOT	8.31	X_OBJ	0.07
SBJ	11.74	P	2.42	X_SBJ	0.09

Table 4: Distribution of all dependency labels (in %).

3.4 Coordination and nested function tags

Because of the conjunctive function tag CNJ, identifying coordination structures is relatively easy. Figure 4 shows constituent and dependency trees for a sentence, *I and he and she left home*, in Korean.

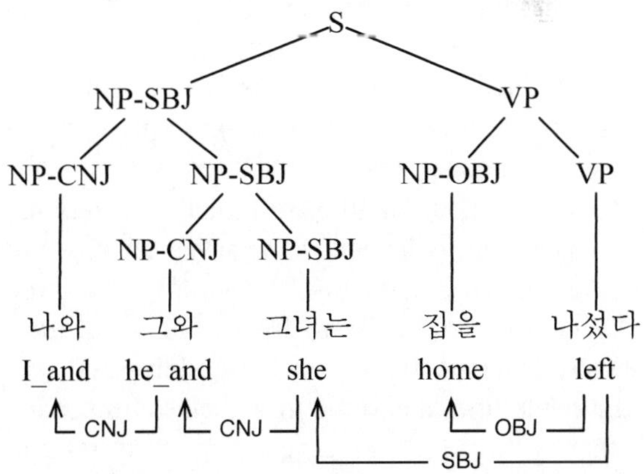

Figure 4: Constituent (top) and dependency (bottom) trees for, *I and he and she left home*, in Korean.

According to our headrules, *she* becomes the head of both *I* and *he*, which is completely acceptable but can cause long-distance dependencies when the coordination chain becomes long. Instead, we make

NN	→	NNG | NNP | SL | SH	VX	→	VX (verb)	SN	→	XSN
NX	→	NNB	AX	→	VX (adjective)	SV	→	XSV
NP	→	NP	DT	→	MM	SJ	→	XSA
NU	→	NR | SN	AD	→	MA*	IJ	→	IC
VI	→	VV (intransitive)	JO	→	J*	NR	→	NF
VT	→	VV (transitive)	EP	→	EP	UK	→	NA | NV | XR
AJ	→	VA | VCN	EM	→	EF | EC | ET*	SY	→	SF | SP | SS | SE | SO | SW
CP	→	VCP	PF	→	XPN			

Table 5: Mappings between POS tags generated by Mach and IMA. In each column, the left-hand and right-hand sides show POS tags generated by Mach and IMA, respectively.

each previous conjunct a dependent of its following conjunct.

Notice that the function tag SBJ is nested twice. In the Sejong Treebank, a nested function tag indicates the head of the phrase, for which we do not need headrules. Thus, whenever a node with a nested function tag is encountered, we take the node as the head of the phrase, regardless of the headrules.

4 Morphological analysis

To generate automatic morphemes and POS tags for input to our dependency parsing model, we run two systems. One is called the Intelligent Morphological Analyzer (IMA), which generates the POS tagset described in Table 1.[6] The other is called Mach that gives a more coarse-grained POS tagset (Shim and Yang, 2002). Table 5 shows mappings between POS tags generated by these systems. Note that these mappings are derived manually by comparing outputs of the two systems.

Both systems are dictionary-based analyzers using vocabularies collected from various sources, including Korean dictionaries. Given a token, these analyzers first generate possible sequences of morphemes, then rank the sequences by adding POS tags with probabilities measured from their training data. Neither of these systems gave the option of retraining their probabilistic models, so we had to verify if their models were not biased to our test data. IMA was distributed before the Sejong Treebank project, so was not trained on the Treebank. We got in touch with the author of Mach and made sure their training model was not biased to our test data.

[6] 지능형 형태소 분석기: http://www.sejong.or.kr/

The reason we use outputs from two different systems is to compare the impact of fine vs. coarse-grained morphologies on dependency parsing in Korean. IMA gives not only richer POS tags but also more fine-grained (segmented) morphemes than Mach. We hypothesize that a richer morphology does not necessarily provide better features for dependency parsing. We evaluate our hypothesis by comparing parsing models trained on morphemes and POS tags generated by these two systems.

5 Dependency parsing

5.1 Parsing algorithm

To build statistical parsing models, we use Choi and Palmer (2011)'s transition-based dependency parsing approach, which has shown state-of-the-art performance in English and Czech. The key idea of this approach is to combine transitions from projective and non-projective dependency parsing algorithms so it can perform projective and non-projective parsing accordingly. As a result, it shows an expected linear time parsing speed for generating both projective and non-projective dependency trees.

Our algorithm uses three lists: λ_1, λ_2, and β. $\lambda_{1,2}$ contain tokens that have been processed and β contains tokens that have not been processed by the algorithm. For each parsing state, the algorithm performs one of the five transitions: LEFT-POP, LEFT-ARC, RIGHT-ARC, NO-ARC, and SHIFT. Transitions are determined by comparing the last token in λ_1, say w_i, with the first token in β, say w_j. After a transition is performed, w_i either moves into λ_2 or gets removed from λ_1, depending on whether or not the oracle predicts the token is needed in later parsing states. w_j is then compared with the last token in

λ_1, that is w_{i-1}. When the oracle predicts there is no token in λ_1 that has a dependency relation with w_j, w_j is removed from β and added to λ_1 along with all other tokens in λ_2. The procedure is repeated with the first token in β, that is w_{j+1}. The algorithm terminates when there is no token left in β.

5.2 Machine learning algorithm

We use Liblinear L2-regularized L1-loss SVM for learning (Hsieh et al., 2008), applying $c = 0.1$ (cost), $e = 0.1$ (termination criterion), $B = 0$ (bias).

5.3 Feature extraction

As mentioned in Section 3.1, each token in our corpora consists of one or many morphemes annotated with different POS tags. This morphology makes it difficult to extract features for dependency parsing. In English, when two tokens, w_i and w_j, are compared for a dependency relation, we extract features like POS tags of w_i and w_j (w_i.pos, w_j.pos), or a joined feature of POS tags between two tokens (w_i.pos+w_j.pos). Since each token is annotated with a single POS tag in English, it is trivial to extract these features. In Korean, each token is annotated with a sequence of POS tags, depending on how morphemes are segmented. It is possible to join all POS tags within a token and treat that as a single tag (e.g., NNP+NNG+JX for the first token in Figure 5); however, these tags usually cause very sparse vectors when used as features.

낙랑공주는	호동왕자를	사랑했다.
*Nakrang*_Princess	*Hodong*_Prince	loved.

낙랑공주는 → 낙랑/NNP+공주/NNG+는/JX

Nakrang + Princess + JX

호동왕자를 → 호동/NNP+왕자/NNG+를/JKO

Hodong + Prince + JKO

사랑했다. → 사랑/NNG+하/XSV+았/EP+다/EF+./SF

Love + XSV + EP + EF + .

Figure 5: Morphological analysis for a sentence, *Princess Nakrang loved Prince Hodong.*, in Korean.

An alternative is to extract the POS tag of only the head morpheme for each token. This prevents the sparsity issue, but we discover that no matter how we choose the head morpheme, it prunes out too many other morphemes helpful for parsing. Thus, as a compromise, we decide to select certain types of morphemes and use only these as features. Table 6 shows the types of morphemes used to extract features for our parsing models.

FS	The first morpheme
LS	The last morpheme before JO | DS | EM
JK	Particles (J* in Table 1)
DS	Derivational suffixes (XS* in Table 1)
EM	Ending markers (E* in Table 1)
PY	The last punctuation, only if there is no other morpheme followed by the punctuation

Table 6: Types of morphemes in each token used to extract features for our parsing models.

Figure 6 shows morphemes extracted from the tokens in Figure 5. For unigrams, these morphemes can be used either individually (e.g., the POS tag of JK for the 1st token is JX) or jointly (e.g., a joined feature of POS tags between LS and JK for the 1st token is NNG+JX) to generate features. From our experiments, features extracted from the JK and EM morphemes are found to be the most useful.

FS	LS	JK	DS	EM	PY
낙랑/NNP	공주/NNG	는/JX	-	-	-
호동/NNP	왕자/NNG	를/JKO	-	-	-
사랑/NNG	-	-	하/XSV	다/EF	./SF

Figure 6: Morphemes extracted from the tokens in Figure 5 with respect to the types in Table 6.

For n-grams where $n > 1$, it is not obvious which combinations of these morphemes across different tokens yield useful features for dependency parsing. Trying out every possible combination is not practical; thus, we restrict our search to only joined features of two morphemes between w_i and w_j, where each morpheme is taken from a different token. It is possible to extend these features to another level, which we will explore in the future.

Table 7 shows a set of individual features extracted from unigrams. w_i is the last token in λ_1 and w_j is the first token in β as described in Section 5.1 (they also represent the i'th and j'th tokens in a sentence, respectively). 'm' and 'p' indicate the form and POS tag of the corresponding morpheme.

	FS	LS	JK	DS	EM	PY
w_i	m,p	m,p	m,p		m,p	m
w_j	m,p	m,p	m,p		m,p	m
w_{i-1}		m	m,p	p	m,p	m
w_{i+1}		m			m,p	m
w_{j-1}	m	p	m,p		m,p	m
w_{j+1}	m,p	m	m	p	p	m

Table 7: Individual features from unigrams.

Table 8 shows a set of joined features extracted from unigrams, w_i and w_j. For instance, a joined feature of forms between FS and LS for the first token in Figure 5 is *Nakrang+Princess*.

	FS	LS	JK
JK	m+m	m+m	
EM	m+m	m+m	m+m

Table 8: Joined features from unigrams, w_i and w_j.

Finally, Table 9 shows a set of joined features extracted from bigrams, w_i and w_j. Each column and row represents a morpheme in w_i and w_j, respectively. 'x' represents a joined feature of POS tags between w_i and w_j. 'y' represents a joined feature between a form of w_i's morpheme and a POS tag of w_j's morpheme. 'z' represents a joined feature between a POS tag of w_i's morpheme and a form of w_j's morpheme. '*' and '+' indicate features used only for fine-grained and coarse-grained morphologies, respectively.

	FS	LS	JK	DS	EM
FS	x	y,z	x^*,y^+,z	z	z
LS	x	x, z	x^*,y^+	x,z	x
JK	x^*,y,z^+	x,y	x^*,y^+,z^+	x,y^+	x^*,y^+
DS	x,z	y	x	x	x, z
EM	x	z	y, z	z	x, z^+

Table 9: Joined features from bigrams, w_i and w_j.

A few other features such as dependency labels of [w_j, the rightmost dependent of w_i, and the leftmost dependent of w_j] are also used. Note that we are considering far fewer tokens than most other dependency parsing approaches (only w_i, w_j, $w_{i\pm1}$, $w_{j\pm1}$). We expect to achieve higher parsing accuracy by considering more tokens; however, this small span of features still gives promising results.

6 Experiments

6.1 Corpora

The Sejong Treebank contains 20 different corpora covering various topics. For our experiments, we group these corpora into 6 genres: Newspaper (NP), Magazine (MZ), Fiction (FI), Memoir (ME), Informative Book (IB), and Educational Cartoon (EC). NP contains newspapers from five different sources talking about world, politics, opinion, etc. MZ contains two magazines about movies and educations. FI contains four fiction texts, and ME contains two memoirs. IB contains six books about science, philosophy, psychology, etc. EC contains one cartoon discussing world history.

Table 10 shows how these corpora are divided into training, development, and evaluation sets. For the development and evaluation sets, we pick one newspaper about art, one fiction text, and one informative book about trans-nationalism, and use each of the first half for development and the second half for evaluation. Note that these development and evaluation sets are very diverse compared to the training data. Testing on such evaluation sets ensures the robustness of our parsing model, which is very important for our purpose because we are hoping to use this model to parse various texts on the web.

	NP	MZ	FI	ME	IB	EC
T	8,060	6,713	15,646	5,053	7,983	1,548
D	2,048	-	2,174	-	1,307	-
E	2,048	-	2,175	-	1,308	-

Table 10: Number of sentences in training (T), development (D), and evaluation (E) sets for each genre.

6.2 Evaluations

To set an upper bound, we first build a parsing model based on gold-standard morphology from the Sejong Treebank, which is considered fine-grained morphology. To compare the impact of fine-grained vs. coarse-grained morphologies, we train two other

	Gold, fine-grained			Auto, fine-grained			Auto, coarse-grained		
	LAS	UAS	LS	LAS	UAS	LS	LAS	UAS	LS
NP	82.58	84.32	94.05	79.61	82.35	91.49	79.00	81.68	91.50
FI	84.78	87.04	93.70	81.54	85.04	90.95	80.11	83.96	90.24
IB	84.21	85.50	95.82	80.45	82.14	92.73	81.43	83.38	93.89
Avg.	**83.74**	**85.47**	**94.57**	**80.43**	**83.01**	**91.77**	**80.14**	**82.89**	**91.99**

Table 11: Parsing accuracies achieved by three models (in %). LAS - labeled attachment score, UAS - unlabeled attachment score, LS - label accuracy score

parsing models, based on the output of IMA, [auto, fine-grained], and the output of Mach, [auto, coarse-grained]. All parsing accuracies achieved by these three models are provided in Table 11.

The [gold, fine-grained] model shows over three points improvement on the average LAS compared to the [auto, fine-grained] model. The [auto, fine-grained] morphology gives an F1-score of 89.59% for morpheme segmentation, and a POS tagging accuracy of 94.66% on correctly segmented morphemes; our parsing model is expected to perform better as the automatic morphological analysis improves. On the other hand, the differences between the [auto, fine-grained] and [auto, coarse-grained] models are small. More specifically, the difference between the average LAS achieved by these two models is statistically significant (McNemar, $p = 0.01$); however, the difference in the average UAS is not statistically significant, and the average LS is actually higher for the [auto, coarse-grained] model.

These results seem to confirm our hypothesis, "a more fine-grained morphology is not necessarily a better morphology for dependency parsing"; however, more careful studies need to be done to verify this. Furthermore, it is only fair to mention that the [auto, fine-grained] model uses a smaller set of features than the [auto, coarse-grained] model (Table 9) because many lexical features can be replaced with POS tag features without compromising accuracy for the [auto, fine-grained] model, but not for the [auto, coarse-grained] model.

It is interesting to see that the numbers are usually high for LS, which shows that our models successfully learn labeling information from morphemes such as case particles or ending markers. All three models show robust results across different genres although the accuracies for NP are significantly lower than the others. We are currently working on the error analysis of why our models perform worse on NP and how to improve accuracy for this genre while keeping the same robustness across the others.

7 Conclusion and future work

There has been much work done on automatic morphological analysis but relatively less work done on dependency parsing in Korean. One major reason is the lack of training data in dependency structure. Here, we present head-percolation rules and heuristics to convert constituent trees in the Sejong Treebank to dependency trees. We believe these head-rules and heuristics can be beneficial for those who want to build statistical dependency parsing models of their own.

As a pioneer of using this dependency Treebank, we focus our effort on feature extraction. Because of rich morphology in Korean, it is not intuitive how to extract features from each token that will be useful for dependency parsing. We suggest a rule-based way of selecting important morphemes and use only these as features to build dependency parsing models. Even with a small span of features, we achieve promising results although there is still much room for improvement.

We will continuously develop our parsing model by testing more features, treating morphemes as individual tokens, adding deterministic rules, etc. We are planning to use our parsing model to improve other NLP tasks in Korean such as machine translation and sentiment analysis.

Acknowledgments

Special thanks are due to Professor Kong Joo Lee of Chungnam National University and Kwangseob Shim of Shungshin Women's University. We gratefully acknowledge the support of the National Science Foundation Grants CISE-IIS-RI-0910992, Richer Representations for Machine Translation. Any opinions, findings, and conclusions or recommendations expressed in this material are those of the authors and do not necessarily reflect the views of the National Science Foundation.

References

Jinho D. Choi and Martha Palmer. 2010. Robust constituent-to-dependency conversion for multiple corpora in english. In *Proceedings of the 9th International Workshop on Treebanks and Linguistic Theories*, TLT'9.

Jinho D. Choi and Martha Palmer. 2011. Getting the most out of transition-based dependency parsing. In *Proceedings of the 49th Annual Meeting of the Association for Computational Linguistics: Human Language Technologies*, ACL:HLT'11, pages 687–692.

Tagyoung Chung, Matt Post, and Daniel Gildea. 2010. Factors affecting the accuracy of korean parsing. In *In Proceedings of NAACL Workshop on Statistical Parsing of Morphologically Rich Languages*, SPMRL'10, pages 49–57.

Hoojung Chung. 2004. *Statistical Korean Dependency Parsing Model based on the Surface Contextual Information*. Ph.D. thesis, Korea University.

Jan Hajič, Massimiliano Ciaramita, Richard Johansson, Daisuke Kawahara, Maria Antònia Martí, Lluís Màrquez, Adam Meyers, Joakim Nivre, Sebastian Padó, Jan Štěpánek, Pavel Straňák, Mihai Surdeanu, Nianwen Xue, and Yi Zhang. 2009. The conll-2009 shared task: Syntactic and semantic dependencies in multiple languages. In *Proceedings of the 13th Conference on Computational Natural Language Learning: Shared Task*, CoNLL'09, pages 1–18.

Chung-hye Han, Benoit Lavoie, Martha Palmer, Owen Rambow, Richard Kittredgc, Tanya Korelsky, Nari Kim, and Myunghee Kim. 2000. Handling structural divergences and recovering dropped arguments in a korean/english machine translation system. In *Proceedings of the Association for Machine Translation in the Arnericas*, AMTA'00.

Chung-hye Han, Na-Rae Han, Eon-Suk Ko, Martha Palmer, and Heejong Yi. 2002. Penn korean treebank: Development and evaluation. In *In Proceedings of the 16th Pacific Asia Conference on Language, Information and Computation*, PACLIC'02.

Na-Rae Han. 2005. Klex: A finite-state transducer lexicon of korean. In *In Proceedings of the 5th International Workshop on Finite-State Methods and Natural Language Processing*.

Cho-Jui Hsieh, Kai-Wei Chang, Chih-Jen Lin, S. Sathiya Keerthi, and S. Sundararajan. 2008. A dual coordinate descent method for large-scale linear svm. In *Proceedings of the 25th international conference on Machine learning (ICML'08)*, pages 408–415.

Richard Johansson and Pierre Nugues. 2007. Extended constituent-to-dependency conversion for english. In *Proceedings of the 16th Nordic Conference of Computational Linguistics*, NODALIDA'07.

Mark Johnson and Ahmet Engin Ural. 2010. Reranking the berkeley and brown parsers. In *Proceedings of the North American Chapter of the Association for Computational Linguistics Conference*, NAACL'10, pages 665–668.

Seung-Shik Kang and Chong-Woo Woo. 2001. Automatic segmentation of words using syllable bigram statistics. In *In Proceedings of the 6th Natural Language Processing Pacific Rim Symposium*, NLPRS'01, pages 729–732.

Kong Joo Lee. 1998. *Probabilistic Parsing of Korean based on Language-Specific Properties*. Ph.D. thesis, Korea Advanced Institute of Science and Technology.

Mitchell P. Marcus, Mary Ann Marcinkiewicz, and Beatrice Santorini. 1993. Building a large annotated corpus of english: The penn treebank. *Computational Linguistics*, 19(2):313–330.

Marie-Catherine de Marneffe, Bill MacCartney, and Christopher D. Manning. 2006. Generating typed dependency parses from phrase structure parses. In *Proceedings of the 5th International Conference on Language Resources and Evaluation*, LREC'06, pages 449–454.

Ryan McDonald, Koby Crammer, and Fernando Pereira. 2005. Online large-margin training of dependency parsers. In *Proceedings of the 43rd Annual Meeting on Association for Computational Linguistics*, pages 91–98.

Joakim Nivre and Ryan McDonald. 2008. Integrating graph-based and transition-based dependency parsers. In *Proceedings of the 46th Annual Meeting of the Association for Computational Linguistics: Human Language Technologies (ACL:HLT'08)*, pages 950–958.

Joakim Nivre and Jens Nilsson. 2005. Pseudo-projective dependency parsing. In *Proceedings of the 43rd Annual Meeting of the Association for Computational Linguistics*, ACL'05, pages 99–106.

Joakim Nivre. 2008. Algorithms for deterministic incremental dependency parsing. *Computational Linguistics*, 34(4):513–553.

Jin-young Oh and Jeong-Won Cha. 2008. Robust korean dependency analysis based on crfs. In *Proceedings of the 20th Annual Conference on Human and Cognitive Language Technology*, HCLT'08, pages 23–28.

Kwangseob Shim and Jaehyung Yang. 2002. Mach : A supersonic korean morphological analyzer. In *Proceedings of the 19th International Conference on Computational Linguistics*, COLING'02, pages 939–945.

Mihai Surdeanu, Richard Johansson, Adam Meyers, Lluís Màrquez, and Joakim Nivre. 2008. The conll-2008 shared task on joint parsing of syntactic and semantic dependencies. In *Proceedings of the 12th Conference on Computational Natural Language Learning: Shared Task*, CoNLL'08, pages 59–177.

Morphological Features for Parsing Morphologically-rich Languages: A Case of Arabic

Jon Dehdari
Department of Linguistics
The Ohio State University
jonsafari@ling.osu.edu

Lamia Tounsi
NCLT, School of Computing
Dublin City University
ltounsi@computing.dcu.ie

Josef van Genabith
CNGL, School of Computing
Dublin City University
josef@computing.dcu.ie

Abstract

We investigate how morphological features in the form of part-of-speech tags impact parsing performance, using Arabic as our test case. The large, fine-grained tagset of the Penn Arabic Treebank (498 tags) is difficult to handle by parsers, ultimately due to data sparsity. However, *ad-hoc* conflations of treebank tags runs the risk of discarding potentially useful parsing information.

The main contribution of this paper is to describe several automated, language-independent methods that search for the optimal feature combination to help parsing. We first identify 15 individual features from the Penn Arabic Treebank tagset. Either including or excluding these features results in 32,768 combinations, so we then apply heuristic techniques to identify the combination achieving the highest parsing performance.

Our results show a statistically significant improvement of 2.86% for vocalized text and 1.88% for unvocalized text, compared with the baseline provided by the Bikel-Bies Arabic POS mapping (and an improvement of 2.14% using product models for vocalized text, 1.65% for unvocalized text), giving state-of-the-art results for Arabic constituency parsing.

1 Introduction

Parsing Arabic is challenging due to its morphological richness and syntactic complexity. In particular, the number of distinct word-forms, the relative freedom with respect to word order, and the information expressed at the level of words make parsing Arabic a difficult task. Previous research established that adapting constituency parsing models developed from English to Arabic (and other languages) is a non-trivial task. Significant effort has been deployed to parse Chinese using the unlexicalized parser of Klein and Manning (2003a,b) with modest performance gains over previous approaches. Due to the specification of head rules, lexicalized parsing models also turned out to be difficult to generalize to other languages: Kulick et al. (2006) describe Arabic parsing results far below English or even Chinese using the Collins parsing model as implemented in the Bikel parser (Bikel, 2004).

In order to side-step the surface representations involved in constituency parsing, several studies have focused on Arabic dependency parsing. The general assumption is that dependency structures are better suited for representing syntactic information for morphologically rich and free-word order languages. However, the results of CoNLL shared tasks on 18 different languages, including Arabic (Nivre et al., 2007a) using either the MaltParser (Nivre et al., 2007b) or the MSTParser (McDonald and Crammer, 2005) suggests that Arabic is nonetheless quite a difficult language to parse[1], leaving open the question as to the effectiveness of dependency parsing for Arabic.

One reason for this ineffectiveness is that many parsers do not make much, if any, use of morphological information (Tsarfaty and Sima'an, 2008; Bengoetxea and Gojenola, 2010; Marton et al., 2010). In fact, many established parsing models do not capture visible morphological information provided by wordforms and thus fail to make important distributional distinctions.

In this paper, using a re-implementation of the Berkeley latent-variable PCFG parser we study how morphological features, as encoded in POS

[1]The quality and size of the treebanks certainly are important issues.

tags, can be learned automatically by modifying the distributional restriction of initial grammar symbols, and how they impact Arabic constituency parsing. We have selected PCFG-LA parsing models because they have been shown to be relatively language-independent with state-of-the-art performance for several languages (Petrov, 2009).

Kulick et al. (2006) reported that extending POS tags with definiteness information helps Arabic PCFG parsing[2], Diab (2007) enriched the POS tagset with gender, number and definiteness to improve Arabic base phrase chunking, and Marton et al. (2010) reported that definiteness, person, number and gender were most helpful for Arabic dependency parsing on predicted tag input. Our method is comparable to this work in terms of the investigation of the morphological features. However, the results are not comparable, as we use a different parsing paradigm, a different form of the treebank, and most importantly, we extend the investigation to use several automated feature selection methods.

Increasing the tagset size can lead to data sparsity and generally exacerbates the problem of unknown words (that is, `word:POS` pairs not attested during training). To overcome this problem, we have experimented with the technique presented in Attia et al. (2010) to handle unknown words (out of vocabulary words – OOV) within a generative parsing model. This method employs a list of heuristics to extract morphological clues from word forms and builds a set of word-classes. Our results show that enriching basic POS tags with morphological information, accompanied by a method for handling unknown words, jointly and statistically significantly improve upon the parsing baseline, which uses the Bikel-Bies collapsed POS tagset (Maamouri et al., 2009) and does not employ morphological information to handle unknown words.

This paper is organized as follows: In Section 2, we review the PCFG-LA parsing model and the dataset for our experiments. Section 3 addresses the different techniques we have applied to explore the morphological features space over the possible combinations, including a comparison with the best morphological features of previous works. In Section 4, we describe the results of applying the parser.

2 General Background

2.1 Parsing Models

Johnson (1998) enriched treebank categories with context information to improve the performance of PCFG parsing, then Klein and Manning (2003b) explored manual and automatic extensions of syntactic categories into a richer category set to enhance PCFG parsing results. Later, Matsuzaki et al. (2005) used unsupervised techniques, known as PCFG-Latent Annotation (PCFG-LA), to learn more fine-grained categories from the treebank. This method involves *splitting* categories of the grammar, leading to a better estimation of their distributional properties. It uses a small amount of random noise to break symmetries. Petrov et al. (2006) proposed *merging* categories that produce a loss in likelihood, and *smoothing* to prevent overfitting.

Petrov (2009) discussed efficient methods for learning and parsing with these latent variable grammars, and demonstrates that this formalism can be adapted to a variety of languages and applications.

An important aspect of this approach is the use of random seeds in the EM initialization points, which was only recently treated in Petrov (2010). Using 16 different seeds (1–16), he saw a range of approximately 0.65% in the F-scores of the development set, and a range of about 0.55% in the F-scores of the test set for English. He also found a Pearson correlation coefficient of 0.34 between the accuracies of the development set of the Peen Treebank and the test set, and therefore suggested less of a reliance on any particular random seed to yield better grammars. This led him to propose combining grammars from several seeds to produce a higher-quality product model.

In this work, we use a re-implementation of the Berkeley parser, which trains a PCFG-LA using the split-merge-smooth procedure and parses using the max-rule algorithm (Petrov et al., 2006; Petrov and Klein, 2007). For our experiments, we apply the split-merge-smooth cycle five times[3]

[2] By comparison, the case feature improved parsing for Czech (Collins et al., 1999) and the combination of the number feature for adjectives and mode feature for verbs improved results for Spanish (Cowan and Collins, 2005).

[3] Petrov et al. (2006) reports that the best grammars for English using the Penn Treebank are obtained by repeating this cycle 5 or 6 times, depending on the test set. We opted for five cycles due to the vast difference in training times: 2

and we parse on sentences of less than or equal to 40 words in length. For English, the Berkeley parser explores n-gram suffixes to distinguish between unknown words ending with *-ing*, *-ed*, *-s*, etc. to assign POS tags. The Berkeley parser does not provide the same methodology to Arabic. For Arabic, we apply the technique used by Attia et al. (2010) for the purpose of classification of unknown words. The methodology uses several heuristics based on the exploration of Arabic prefixes, suffixes and templates, and then maps unknown words onto 26 classes.

We present our final experiment on the test set and all intermediate experiments on the development set.

2.2 Corpus: Arabic Penn Treebank

We use the Penn Arabic Treebank (ATB Part3v3.2: Maamouri et al., 2009) and apply the usual treebank split (80% training, 10% development, 10% test; Kulick et al. (2006)).[4] The ATB uses written Modern Standard Arabic newswire and follows the style of the English Penn-II treebank (Marcus et al., 1994). The ATB consists of 12,628 parsed sentences which provides gold segmented, gold vocalized and gold annotated text. More precisely, a tokenized Arabic word is separated from its prefixes and suffixes and it is also segmented to morphemes. For example, the Arabic word الْيَوْمُ is vocalized, segmented and transliterated using Buckwalter transliteration to `Al+yawom+u` (the + day + NOM).

2.3 Part-Of-Speech Tagset

The POS tagset in the ATB covers nouns, pronouns, adjectives, verbs, adverbs, prepositions, interjections, particles, conjunctions, and subordinating conjunctions. This tagset uses 78 atomic components, such as: `ABBREV` for abbreviation, `ACC` for accusative case and `ADJ` for adjective. While there are theoretically hundreds of thousands of full ATB-style POS tags (Habash and Rambow, 2005), only 498 full tags occur in the above-mentioned version of the ATB. For example, `Al+dawol+atayoni` ("the states") receives the following tag `DET+NOUN+NSUFF_FEM_DU_GEN`, annotating a definite, feminine, dual noun in the genitive case.

From this tagset we derive all our experiments. We have identified 15 morphological features from those present in the treebank[5], and our method, based on these features, searches for the optimal POS tagset for parsing the ATB. Table 1 lists these features used in our research. No capitalization is used in Arabic orthography and named entities are often tagged as regular nouns. For this reason we consider "proper noun" as a morphological feature (feature 11) .

1	Determiner	Presence of the prefix *al-* for nouns
2	Person	First person, second person, third person
3	Number	Singular, dual, and plural
4	Aspect	Perfective, imperfective and imperative
5	Voice	Active and passive
6	Mood	Indicative, subjunctive and jussive
7	Gender	Masculine and feminine
8	State	Construct state (*iḍāfa*)
9	Case	Nominative, accusative and genitive. The ATB suffers from accusative-genitive case under-specification for feminine and masculine plurals
10	Definiteness	Noun can be definite even if it does not start with *al-*, e.g. proper nouns are assumed to be inherently definite
11	Proper noun	Name of people, places, and organizations
12	Genitive clitics	Possessive pronouns
13	Negation	Negative markers
14	Particles	Emphatic, restrictive, negative, interrogative, focus, connective, verbal, response conditional
15	Future	Presence of the future prefix *sa-* for verbs

Table 1: Morphological features in Arabic

We investigate two directions to find optimal tagsets, as follows:

Direction 1: starts from ATB top tagset (|498|) and reduces the size of the tagset by excluding the features that hurt parsing performance. In our initial set of experiments, we trained and parsed 15 different configurations, each configuration starting from the top tagset, then excluding one feature. For instance, training and parsing after excluding feature 9, case, produces the best results from the first level, $A_{\top-1}$ (see Table 1).

hours vs. 8 hours, with F-scores being almost the same.

[4]Specifically for every 10 sentences, the first 8 go into the training set, the 9th sentence go into the test set, and the 10th sentence into the dev set.

[5]Annotation guidelines at `http://projects.ldc.upenn.edu/ArabicTreebank`

Direction 2: In order to produce the bottom ATB tagset (|27|), we exclude all 15 features. Then we include one feature at a time, giving us another level $A_{\perp+1}$. For instance, training and parsing after including feature 12, genitive clitics, gives the best results compared with other individual features (see Table 1).

These approaches are further developed in Section 3.

3 Part-Of-Speech and Morphological Features

Since Arabic words are highly inflected, there is a complex interaction between the morphology and the syntax. Thus parsers that have morphological information on hand can make better-informed decisions regarding parse trees. The ATB represents morphological features in the form of complex part-of-speech tags. Features representing agglutinated morphemes are likewise agglutinated in the POS tags, separated by a "+" symbol. Features representing fused morphemes are likewise fused in the POS tags, making feature extraction or conflation particularly challenging.

Due to the large size of the original ATB tagset (|498|), many Arabic parsing systems use the Bikel-Bies POS mapping (Bikel, 2004), which maps the original ATB tagset onto a small, PTB-style tagset of 37 tags, discarding almost all morphological features that are not also present in the English PTB.

But are some of the morphological features helpful in parsing Arabic? Kulick et al. (2006) showed this to be the case. They preserved two morphological features (Determiner and Demonstrative) that would otherwise have been lost in the existing Bikel-Bies POS mapping, and achieved a higher F-score. However, Arabic has many morphological features. We have identified fifteen sets of morphological features in the ATB, such as voice, mood, and grammatical gender (see Table 1).

Including or excluding these features allows for 32,768 combinations (2^{15}). Training and parsing all of these combinations is prohibitively expensive, so an alternative is to use various heuristics on the powerset of the features, some of which are described below. Many of these methods rely on an initial heuristic function $h_{\perp+1}(x)$, which is derived by ranking the results of using individual features. The antichain $A_{\perp+1}$ in Figure 1 gives

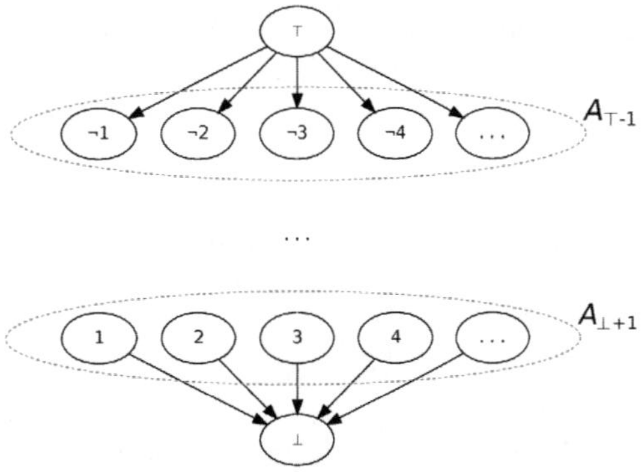

Figure 1: The top node $\top$ represents the tagset containing all ATB morphological features, and the bottom node $\perp$ represents the tagset excluding all morphological features. Each node in the antichain $A_{\top-1}$ excludes one morphological feature, and each node in the antichain $A_{\perp+1}$ includes one morphological feature.

$h_{\perp+1}(x)$. Its dual, $h_{\top-1}(x)$, is derived by ranking the results of not using individual features. The antichain $A_{\top-1}$ in Figure 1 gives $h_{\top-1}(x)$.

We investigated the following automated methods to find the tagset giving the best parse results:

Non-iterative: A non-iterative best-first algorithm that successively folds-in the next-best feature. Thus if there are 5 features ranked individually from best to worst as $\langle 4, 1, 5, 3, 2\rangle$, then there are 4 tagsets to explore: $\{4, 1\}$ $\{4, 1, 5\}$ $\{4, 1, 5, 3\}$ $\{4, 1, 5, 3, 2\}$. After $h_{\perp+1}(x)$ is defined, the algorithm does not require results from previous steps, and thus can be run in parallel. At most f–1 parses are run, where f is the number of features. The dual of this uses $h_{\top-1}(x)$ to rank the results of excluding exactly one feature.

Greedy-iterative: An iterative, greedy best-first search algorithm with a single heuristic function throughout. We use the heuristic function $h_{\perp+1}(x)$ to rank the results of including exactly one feature, then iteratively fold in the next feature and retain it only if it achieves a higher score. This requires f–1 iterations after $h_{\perp+1}(x)$ is obtained. This method was used by Marton et al. (2010) and Marton et al. (2011). The dual of this uses $h_{\top-1}(x)$ to rank the results of excluding exactly one feature.

Merged: The previous two methods can instead use a different heuristic function by merging the results of $A_{\bot+1}$ with the results of $A_{\top-1}$. This potentially provides more robust results than either one individually, without requiring any additional iterations. The merge function $M(f)$ is defined as:

$$M(f) = (S_{\top} - S_{\neg f}) + (S_f - S_{\bot})$$

where S_f is the F-score of including a given feature f. The results of $M(f)$ are ordered to provide the merged heuristic function $h_m(x)$.

Backtrack: An iterative, best-first backtracking algorithm that updates its heuristic function at each iteration. Whereas the previous algorithm uses a single heuristic function throughout (such as $h_{\bot+1}(x)$), for this algorithm the next feature chosen is decided by $h_i(x)$, which is based upon the results of the current iteration i. The most helpful feature at each iteration is chosen. After exhausting this path, it will backtrack, discarding the most-recently added feature and instead revisit $h_{i-1}(x)$. The dual of this uses $h_{\top-1}(x)$ to rank the results of excluding exactly one feature, and starts from the top.

Like beam-stack search (Zhou and Hansen, 2005), this algorithm has the advantage of being an anytime search algorithm, which quickly finds good solutions while still finding a globally optimal solution. However, this algorithm is much simpler conceptually than beam-stack search, it proceeds best-first, and the beam width is determined by the number of unused features.

4 Experimental Results

We have experimented with the strategies presented in section 3. All our feature selection experiments are based on the results of vocalized no-tag parsing on the development set where the parser assigns the tags learned during the training phase. However we also provide the results of gold tag and unvocalized no-tag parsing in our final experiments. We measure quality and coverage of the output trees using the standard EVALB (Satoshi and Collins, 1997).

The initial results on parsing are presented in Table 2. These results describe the first stage of traversing the powerset of features. Only one feature is included (in $A_{\bot+1}$) or excluded (in $A_{\top-1}$) at a time. The Bikel-Bies POS tagset included in the Penn Arabic Treebank part 3 v3.2 represents our baseline.[6] At this stage, we use the obtained F-scores to derive our initial $h(x)$ for all methods, since we are interested in measuring relative improvements when changing POS tagsets.

Bikel-Bies POS	81.33	
$\top$	81.99	
$\bot$	81.98	
Features	$\mathbf{A}_{\top-1}$	$\mathbf{A}_{\bot+1}$
1 Determiner	81.52	82.33
2 Person	81.80	81.46
3 Number	81.64	81.56
4 Aspect	82.00	81.81
5 Voice	81.99	82.57
6 Mood	82.21	82.27
7 Gender	82.06	82.15
8 State	81.60	82.07
9 Case	**83.00**	81.68
10 Definiteness	82.10	82.41
11 Proper noun	82.13	82.27
12 Genitive clitics	82.26	**82.69**
13 Negation	81.71	82.42
14 Particles	81.20	82.61
15 Future	81.70	82.25

Table 2: Parsing results (F-score) for including features 1–15 in $A_{\bot+1}$ and excluding features 1–15 in $A_{\top-1}$.

The results presented in Table 3 correspond to the non-iterative method. Line 6 shows that the improvement for this configuration is mainly due to adding feature 1 (determiner) and lines 7–8 show that feature 11 (proper noun) is helpful only when it is associated with feature 6 (mood).

Table 4 presents the results of the greedy-iterative method using a single heuristic function (left) and a merged heuristic function (right). The method using single heuristic function was also employed by Marton et al. (2010). Grey rows indicate that the feature decreased the F-score, and thus was discarded. The number of iterations with this algorithm is fixed at f–1 after the initial heuristic function is obtained, where f is the number of morphological features. We can observe that the features 11,13 (proper noun & negation) work together to produce the highest jump in the score.

In contrast with the results of Marton et al.

[6] This tagset has 37 unique tags in the treebank.

$\perp$	81.98
$\{12\}$	82.69
$\{12, 14\}$	82.36
$\{12, 14, 5\}$	82.48
$\{12, 14, 5, 13\}$	82.20
$\{12, 14, 5, 13, 10\}$	82.49
$\{12, 14, 5, 13, 10, 1\}$	82.94
$\{12, 14, 5, 13, 10, 1, 11\}$	82.78
$\mathbf{\{12, 14, 5, 13, 10, 1, 11, 6\}}$	**83.02**
$\{12, 14, 5, 13, 10, 1, 11, 6, 15\}$	82.54
...	...

Table 3: Parsing results for the non-iterative method. The tagset with highest F-score contains genitive clitics, particles, voice, negation, definiteness, determiner, proper noun, and mood. The improvement over the baseline is statistically significant.

$\perp$	81.98	$\perp$	81.98
$\{12\}$	82.69	$\{10\}$	82.41
$\{12, 14\}$	82.36	$\{10, 13\}$	82.97
$\{12, 5\}$	82.44	$\{10, 13, 14\}$	82.38
$\{12, 13\}$	82.24	$\{10, 13, 1\}$	82.65
$\{12, 10\}$	81.79	$\{10, 13, 8\}$	82.44
$\{12, 1\}$	81.80	$\{10, 13, 3\}$	82.22
$\mathbf{\{12, 11\}}$	**82.87**	$\{10, 13, 7\}$	82.48
$\{12, 11, 6\}$	82.33	$\{10, 13, 5\}$	82.00
$\{12, 11, 15\}$	82.59	$\mathbf{\{10, 13, 11\}}$	**83.07**
$\{12, 11, 7\}$	81.83	$\{10, 13, 11, 12\}$	82.378
$\{12, 11, 8\}$	82.01	$\{10, 13, 11, 6\}$	82.38
$\{12, 11, 4\}$	81.98	$\{10, 13, 11.2\}$	82.45
$\{12, 11, 9\}$	82.19	$\{10, 13, 11, 4\}$	82.89
$\{12, 11, 3\}$	82.40	$\{10, 13, 11, 15\}$	82.30
$\{12, 11, 2\}$	81.92	$\{10, 13, 11, 9\}$	82.56

Table 4: Parsing results for the greedy-best-first method with a single heuristic, using $h_{\perp+1}(x)$ in the left table and $h_m(x)$ in the right table. The tagset with highest F-score on the left contains genitive clitics and proper noun markers. However, the improvement over the baseline is not statistically significant. The tagset with highest F-score on the right contains definiteness, negation and proper noun markers. In this case, the improvement over the baseline is statistically significant.

(2010), the so-called ϕ-features (person, number, gender) did not contribute to a higher score in our experiments. We believe this is in part because morphological features are represented as atomic tags in the Penn Arabic Treebank. Generative parsers that use this style of treebank typically do not analyze individual features and make use of them in determining agreement relationships. On the other hand, the CoNLL-X format[7] provides a field where morphological features are specified individually. This encourages dependency parsers to inspect individual components of a tag, and make use of specific features when helpful. The CoNLL-X format is used by most dependency parsers, including the MaltParser used in Marton et al. (2010).

The landscape of the search space contains many local maxima, which can prevent (non-backtracking) greedy algorithms from exploring paths that eventually lead to high scores. Consider the case below:

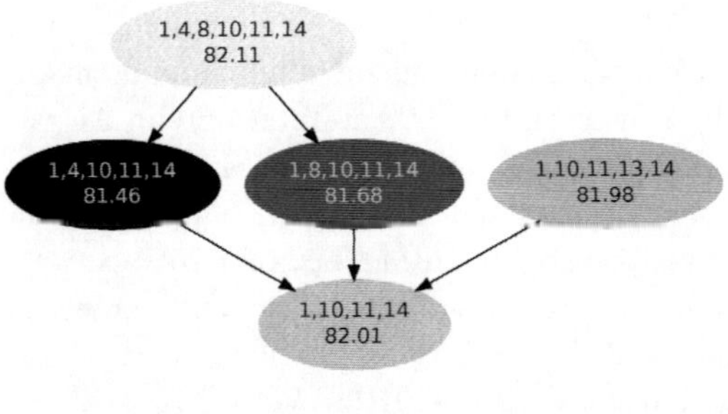

A greedy algorithm arriving at feature combination 1,10,11,14 moving upward will pursue an unfruitful 1,10,11,13,14, never arriving at the highest feature combination 1,4,8,10,11,14. Features 4 (aspect) and 8 (state) may work together to provide a useful distinction for parsing that individually would otherwise only increase sparsity.

Table 5 gives the results of using the best-first with backtracking algorithm. We join the highest-ranked individual feature (12: genitive clitics) with all other individual features (i.e. $\{12, 1\}$ $\{12, 2\}$ $\{12, 3\}$ ...), and select the combination achieving the highest F-score ($\{12, 11\}$). The initial heuristic function $h_{\perp+1}(x)$ is used only in the first iteration (to select feature 12 in our case). Afterward, we join the resulting set with all other remaining individual features (i.e. $\{12, 11, 1\}$ $\{12, 11, 2\}$ $\{12, 11, 3\}$ ...), and select the combination achieving the highest score. With each iteration, the number of remaining features is decremented by one. While this algorithm is exhaustive, we have not explored all possible combinations.

We also investigated a probabilistic search algorithm to see how well it could overcome the challenges posed by many local maxima. Using simulated annealing (Kirkpatrick et al., 1983), we performed 50 experiments, with 50 cycles each. The mean of the final dev-set F-scores was 82.84,

[7] http://nextens.uvt.nl/~conll/#dataformat

$\perp$	81.98
$\{12\}$	82.69
...	
$\{12, 11\}$	82.87
...	
$\{12, 11, 13\}$	82.60
...	
$\mathbf{\{12, 11, 13, 1\}}$	**83.16**
...	

Table 5: Parsing results for the best-first with backtracking method. The improvement of the score over the baseline is statistically significant. The best feature combination includes the following features: genitive clitics, proper noun, negation, and determiner. The cardinality of the best-performing tagset is 41.

with a standard deviation of 0.21 . As is usually the case, the cooling schedule played an important role in the results. We evaluated three different cooling schedules, and found that the slowest one resulted in many low scores, given the same number of cycles. This was due to the higher probability of jumping to a higher energy state later in the experiment. This is often advantageous given a large number of cycles, however we are limited to fewer cycles due to the high cost of performing each training/parsing cycle.

We observed that simulated annealing usually required many more cycles to find a good score (e.g. higher than 82.40) than the previous search methods described. This was due to their differences in starting points and movement strategies. The previous methods started from the bottom and added potentially helpful features, in various ways. On the other hand, simulated annealing started at a random location in the powerset, and moved stochastically. The differences in the results indicate that many of the high scores lie relatively near the bottom, whereas there is much greater uncertainty in the middle of the feature powerset.

For comparative purposes, Table 6 presents the results obtained by using the most helpful features proposed in two previous works.[8] The Determiner feature in the first row was added by Kulick et al. (2006) to the Bikel-Bies POS tagset, using the Bikel parser. The features in the last two rows were determined by using the MaltParser with the Columbia Arabic Treebank (CATiB: Habash and Roth, 2009) and discussed in Marton et al. (2010).

[8]Using the same setup as in the other experiments in this paper (eg. PCFG-LA parser and ATB3v3.2).

While the case feature (9) helped their gold-tag parsing, it was not helpful for either vocalized or unvocalized parsing in our experiments. Case markings in Arabic exhibit ambiguity with certain noun forms—there are particular instances where both the genitive and accusative endings are the same, such as the duals and masculine plurals. Related to this is the imperfect alignment in Arabic between true grammatical function and morphological case markings (in vocalized and to a lesser extent unvocalized text).

As expected, these features do not achieve the highest overall F-score. Given the variability with different parsers, annotation schemes, evaluation metrics, etc., it should not be surprising that there is no "universally-best" tagset for a language, but rather a tagset optimized for a given task. For example, while the gender feature has not benefited PCFG-LA parsing in our experiments, it could be vitally important for MT applications. But these systems must be able to readily access these individual features, or they may not be utilized.

Kulick +Determiner	$\{1\}$	82.33
Marton best predicted tags	$\{1, 2, 3, 7\}$	79.23
Marton best gold tags	$\{8, 9\}$	82.40

Table 6: F-scores on tag combinations proposed by previous investigations, using the PCFG-LA parser.

Tables 7 and 8 present the final results on the vocalized development set and test set. We applied significance tests on all the results in these tables, and significantly-improved F-scores are indicated with asterisks. The no-tag column gives F-scores when the parser was not given any part-of-speech information in the test (or dev) set at all—just the text to be parsed. Tables 9 and 10 present the final results on the unvocalized development set and test set.

We have also investigated multiple, automatically-learned grammars that differ only in the random seed used to initialize the EM learning algorithm. We explored seeds 1–50, and found a statistically significant difference of 1.24% between the highest EM initialization seed and the lowest, and decided to pursue combining seeds into product models (Petrov, 2010). We explored different *seed combinations* (rather than feature combinations, as before) to form the product models of the baseline and the highest feature combination found in the development set. Using the non-iterative search method described in section 3, we took the highest-scoring 16 seeds from seeds 1–50 and successively folded-in the next-best seed. Figure 2 shows that the F-scores of the vocalized models tend to level off after incorporating the four highest-scoring seeds. The unvocalized counterparts see continued gradual improvements with larger product models, possibly due to less data sparsity.

Tagset	No-tag	Gold
Bikel-Bies Baseline	81.33	85.36
Bikel-Bies + OOV	82.23**	85.59*
{12, 11, 13, 1} + OOV	83.16***	85.94***
Bikel-Bies Baseline + product models	83.70	87.02
{12, 11, 13, 1}+OOV+product models	**84.40***	87.52***

Table 7: Final F-scores on the *vocalized development set* for the best feature combination, and handling unknown words. The best feature combination included the following features: genitive clitics, proper noun, negation, and determiner. Statistically significant with *=$p < 0.05$, **=$p < 0.01$, ***= $p < 0.001$

Tagset	No-tag	Gold
Bikel-Bies Baseline	80.69	85.03
Bikel-Bies + OOV	82.45***	85.29
{12, 11, 13, 1} + OOV	83.55***	85.89*
Bikel-Bies Baseline + product models	82.89	87.10
{12, 11, 13, 1}+OOV+product models	**85.03***	87.57***

Table 8: Final F-scores on the *vocalized test set* for the best feature combination, and handling unknown words. Statistically significant with *=$p < 0.05$, **=$p < 0.01$, ***= $p < 0.001$

Tagset	No-tag	Gold
Bikel-Bies Baseline	80.08	85.12
Bikel-Bies + OOV	81.44***	85.42
{12, 11, 13, 1} + OOV	82.30***	86.67**
Bikel-Bies Baseline + product models	82.33	87.49
{12, 11, 13, 1}+OOV+product models	**84.10***	87.89

Table 9: Final F-scores on the *unvocalized development set* for the best feature combination, and handling unknown words. The best feature combination included the following features: genitive clitics, proper noun, negation, and determiner. Statistically significant with *=$p < 0.05$, **=$p < 0.01$, ***= $p < 0.001$

Tagset	No-tag	Gold
Bikel-Bies Baseline	80.26	85.61
Bikel-Bies + OOV	80.72	85.83
{12, 11, 13, 1} + OOV	82.14***	86.20
Bikel-Bies Baseline + product models	81.69	87.23
{12, 11, 13, 1}+OOV+product models	**83.34***	87.38

Table 10: Final F-scores on the *unvocalized test set* for the best feature combination, and handling unknown words. Statistically significant with *=$p < 0.05$, **=$p < 0.01$, ***= $p < 0.001$

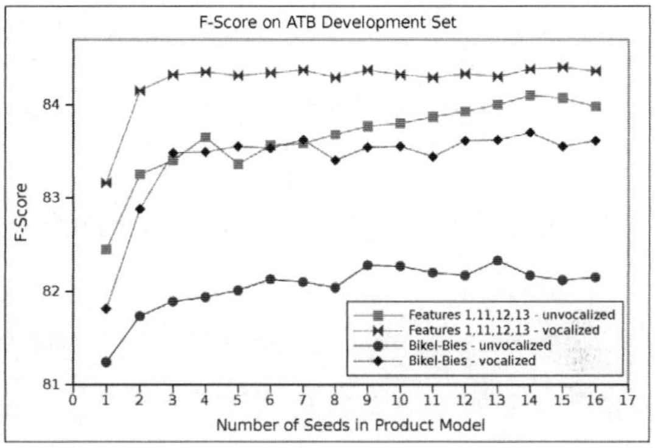

Figure 2: Development set F-scores using product models from multiple grammars.

5 Conclusion

This paper focuses on finding the best use of morphological features for PCFG-LA parsing. We identify 15 morphological features and use the original Penn Arabic Treebank POS tagset (|498|) and a shallow version that excludes all morphological features (|27|), and apply feature inclusion or exclusion to calculate the optimal feature combination for Arabic parsing. We show that using morphological information helps parsing even though it results in a larger tagset. In order to diminish the impact of the newly created POS tags on unknown words, we use a list of Arabic signatures to differentiate between these unknown words when assigning POS tags based on string examination.

We have applied several search methods to find the feature combination that improves grammar quality the most, using **i)** a non-iterative best-first search algorithm, **ii)** an iterative, greedy best-first search algorithm with a single heuristic function, **iii)** an iterative, best-first with backtracking search algorithm, and **iv)** simulated annealing.

The best-first with backtracking algorithm has provided the best results, achieving state-of-the-art

F-scores of 85.03 for vocalized ATB no-tag parsing and 83.34 for unvocalized ATB no-tag parsing, significant improvements of 2.17% and 1.88% over the baseline. These results, together with the scores of the other search algorithms, suggest that the optimal morphological feature combination for this task involves including just a few features. Three out of the four features from our optimal tagset occur in noun phrases. Since noun phrases are so common[9], features that can help parse just these phrases appear to have a great impact on overall F-scores.

We have also performed experiments using features highlighted in previous studies on different parsing models, and have shown that considering only one tagset for a language does not provide optimal scores.

Acknowledgements

This research is funded by Enterprise Ireland (PC/09/037). We would like to thank Chris Brew, Mike White, William Schuler, Jennifer Foster, Joseph Le Roux, Eric Fosler-Lussier, Dennis Mehay, Andy Plummer, and anonymous reviewers for all their very helpful suggestions.

References

Attia, M., Foster, J., Hogan, D., Le Roux, J., Tounsi, L., and van Genabith, J. (2010). Handling unknown words in statistical latent-variable parsing models for Arabic, English and French. In *NAACL/ HLT Workshop on Statistical Parsing of Morphologically Rich Languages*, pages 67–75.

Bengoetxea, K. and Gojenola, K. (2010). Application of different techniques to dependency parsing of Basque. In *NAACL/ HLT Workshop on Statistical Parsing of Morphologically Rich Languages*, pages 37–39.

Bikel, D. (2004). *On the Parameter Space of Generative Lexicalized Parsing Models*. PhD thesis, University of Pennslyvania.

Collins, M., Hajič, J., Ranshaw, L., and Tillman, C. (1999). A statistical parser for Czech. In *Proceedings of the Annual Meeting of the Association for Computational Linguistics*.

[9] NP's comprise 58% of all non-terminals in the treebank that we used. They are more than five times more frequent than the next most common non-terminal (PP).

Cowan, B. and Collins, M. (2005). Morphology and reranking for the statistical parsing of Spanish. In *Proceedings of Human Language Technology Conference and Conference on Empirical Methods in Natural Language Processing*, pages 795–802, Vancouver, British Columbia, Canada. Association for Computational Linguistics.

Diab, M. T. (2007). Improved Arabic base phrase chunking with a new enriched POS tag set. In *ACL Workshop on Computational Approaches to Semitic Languages: Common Issues and Resources*, pages 89–96.

Habash, N. and Rambow, O. (2005). Arabic tokenization, part-of-speech tagging and morphological disambiguation in one fell swoop. In *Proceedings of the 43rd Annual Meeting on Association for Computational Linguistics*, ACL '05, pages 573–580, Stroudsburg, PA, USA. Association for Computational Linguistics.

Habash, N. and Roth, R. (2009). CATiB: The Columbia Arabic Treebank. In *Proceedings of the ACL-IJCNLP 2009 Conference Short Papers*, pages 221–224, Suntec, Singapore. Association for Computational Linguistics.

Johnson, M. (1998). PCFG models of linguistic tree representations. *Computational Linguistics*, 24(4):613–632.

Kirkpatrick, S., Gelatt, C. D. J., and Vecchi, M. P. (1983). Optimization by simulated annealing. *Science*, 220(4598):671–680.

Klein, D. and Manning, C. (2003a). A* parsing: fast exact viterbi parse selection. In *Proceedings of the North American Association for Association for Computational Linguistics*.

Klein, D. and Manning, C. (2003b). Accurate unlexicalized parsing. In *Proceedings of the 41st Annual Meeting of the ACL*, pages 423–430.

Kulick, S., Gabbard, R., and Marcus, M. (2006). Parsing the Arabic Treebank: Analysis and improvements. In *Proceedings of the Treebanks and Linguistic Theories Conference (TLT-2006)*, pages 31–42, Prague, Czech Republic.

Maamouri, M., Bies, A., and Kulic, S. (2009). Creating a methodology for large-scale correction of treebank annotation: The case of the Arabic treebank. In Choukri, K. and Maegaard,

B., editors, *MEDAR Second International Conference on Arabic Language Resources and Tools, Egypt*.

Marcus, M., Kim, G., Marcinkiewicz, M. A., MacIntyre, R., Bies, A., Ferguson, M., Katz, K., and Schasberger, B. (1994). The Penn Treebank: Annotating predicate argument structure. In *Proceedings of the 1994 ARPA Speech and Natural Language Workshop*, pages 114–119, Princeton, NJ, USA.

Marton, Y., Habash, N., and Rambow, O. (2010). Improving Arabic dependency parsing with lexical and inflectional morphological features. In *Proceedings of the NAACL HLT 2010 First Workshop on Statistical Parsing of Morphologically-Rich Languages*, pages 13–21, Los Angeles, CA, USA. Association for Computational Linguistics.

Marton, Y., Habash, N., and Rambow, O. (2011). Improving Arabic dependency parsing with form-based and functional morphological features. In *Proceedings of the 49th Annual Meeting of the Association for Computational Linguistics: Human Language Technologies*, pages 1586–1596, Portland, Oregon, USA. Association for Computational Linguistics.

Matsuzaki, T., Miyao, Y., and Tsujii, J. (2005). Probabilistic CFG with latent annotations. In *Proceedings of the 43rd Annual Meeting of the ACL*, pages 75–82, Ann Arbor, MI, USA.

McDonald, R. and Crammer, K. (2005). Online large-margin training of dependency parsers. In *Proceedings of the Annual Meeting of the Association for Computational Linguistics*.

Nivre, J., Hall, J., Kübler, S., McDonald, R., Nilsson, J., Riedel, S., and Yuret, D. (2007a). The CoNLL 2007 shared task on dependency parsing. In *Proceedings of the CoNLL Shared Task Session of EMNLP-CoNLL 2007*, pages 915–932, Prague, Czech Republic. Association for Computational Linguistics.

Nivre, J., Hall, J., Nilsson, J., Chanev, A., Eryıgıt, G., Kübler, S., Marinov, S., and Marsi, E. (2007b). Maltparser: A language-independent system for data-driven dependency parsing. *Natural Language Engineering*, 13(2):95–135.

Petrov, S. (2009). *Coarse-to-Fine Natural Language Processing*. PhD thesis, University of California at Berkeley, Berkeley, CA, USA.

Petrov, S. (2010). Products of random latent variable grammars. In *Human Language Technologies: The 2010 Annual Conference of the North American Chapter of the Association for Computational Linguistics (NAACL)*, pages 19–27, Los Angeles, CA, USA. Association for Computational Linguistics.

Petrov, S., Barrett, L., Thibaux, R., and Klein, D. (2006). Learning accurate, compact and interpretable tree annotation. In *Proceedings of the 21st International Conference on Computational Linguistics and the 44th Annual Meeting of the ACL*, Sydney, Australia.

Petrov, S. and Klein, D. (2007). Improved inference for unlexicalized parsing. In *Proceedings of HLT-NAACL*, Rochester, NY, USA.

Satoshi, S. and Collins, M. (1997). Evalb bracket scoring program.

Tsarfaty, R. and Sima'an, K. (2008). Relational-realizational parsing. In *Proceedings of Conference on Computational Linguistics (CoLing)*, pages 18–22.

Zhou, R. and Hansen, E. A. (2005). Beam-stack search: Integrating backtracking with beam search. In *Proceedings of the International Conference on Automated Planning and Scheduling (ICAPS)*, pages 90–98, Monterey, CA, USA.

French parsing enhanced with a word clustering method based on a syntactic lexicon

Anthony Sigogne
Université Paris-Est, LIGM
sigogne@univ-mlv.fr

Matthieu Constant
Université Paris-Est, LIGM
mconstan@univ-mlv.fr

Éric Laporte
Université Paris-Est, LIGM
laporte@univ-mlv.fr

Abstract

This article evaluates the integration of data extracted from a French syntactic lexicon, the Lexicon-Grammar (Gross, 1994), into a probabilistic parser. We show that by applying clustering methods on verbs of the French Treebank (Abeillé et al., 2003), we obtain accurate performances on French with a parser based on a Probabilistic Context-Free Grammar (Petrov et al., 2006).

1 Introduction

Syntactic lexicons are rich language resources that may contain useful data for parsers like subcategorisation frames, as it provides, for each lexical entry, information about its syntactic behaviors. Many works on probabilistic parsing studied the use of a syntactic lexicon. We can cite Lexical-Functional Grammar [LFG] (O'Donovan et al., 2005; Schluter and Genabith, 2008), Head-Driven Phrase Structure Grammar [HPSG] (Carroll and Fang, 2004) and Probabilistic Context-Free Grammars [PCFG] (Briscoe and Carroll, 1997; Deoskar, 2008). The latter has incorporated valence features of verbs to PCFGs and observe slight improvements on global performances. However, the incorporation of syntactic data on part-of-speech tags increases the effect of data sparseness, especially when the PCFG grammar is extracted from a small treebank[1]. (Deoskar, 2008) was forced to reestimate parameters of his grammar with an unsupervised algorithm applied on a large raw corpus. In the case of French, this observation can be linked to experiments described in (Crabbé and Candito, 2008) where POS tags are augmented with some syntactic functions[2]. Results have shown a huge decrease on performances.

The problem of data sparseness for PCFG is also lexical. The richer the morphology of a language, the sparser the lexicons built from a treebank will be for that language. Nevertheless, the effect of lexical data sparseness can be reduced by word clustering algorithms. Inspired by the clustering method of (Koo et al., 2008), (Candito and Crabbé, 2009; Candito et al., 2010) have shown that by replacing each word of the corpus by automatically obtained clusters of words, they can improve a PCFG parser on French. They also created two other clustering methods. A first method consists in a step of *desinflection* that removes some inflexional marks of words which are considered less important for parsing. Another method consists in replacing each word by the combination of its POS tag and lemma. Both methods improve significantly performances.

In this article, we propose a clustering method based on data extracted from a syntactic lexicon, the Lexicon-Grammar. This lexicon offers a classification of lexical items into tables, each table being identifiable by its unique identifier. A lexical item is a lemmatized form which can be present in one or more tables depending on its meaning and its syntactic behaviors. The clustering method consists in replacing a verb by the combination of its POS tag and its tables identifiers. The goal of this article is to show that a syntactic lexicon, like the Lexicon-

[1]Data sparseness implies the difficulty of estimating probabilities of rare rules extracted from the corpus.

[2]There were 28 original POS tags and each can be combined with one of the 8 syntactic functions.

Grammar, which is not originally developed for parsing algorithms, is able to improve performances of a probabilistic parser.
In section 2 and 3, we describe the probabilistic parser and the treebank, namely the French Treebank, used in our experiments. In section 4, we describe more precisely previous work on clustering methods. Section 5 introduces the Lexicon-Grammar. We detail information contained in this lexicon that can be used in the parsing process. Then, in section 6, we present methods to integrate this information into parsers and, in section 7, we describe our experiments and discuss the obtained results.

2 Non-lexicalized PCFG parser

The probabilistic parser, used into our experiments, is the Berkeley Parser[3] (called BKY thereafter) (Petrov et al., 2006). This parser is based on a PCFG model which is non-lexicalized. The main problem of non-lexicalized context-free grammars is that nonterminal symbols encode too general information which weakly discriminates syntactic ambiguities. The benefit of BKY is to try to solve the problem by generating a grammar containing complex symbols. It follows the principle of latent annotations introduced by (Matsuzaki et al., 2005). It consists in iteratively creating several grammars, which have a tagset increasingly complex. For each iteration, a symbol of the grammar is splitted in several symbols according to the different syntactic behaviors of the symbol that occur into a treebank. Parameters of the latent grammar are estimated with an algorithm based on Expectation-Maximisation (EM). In the case of French, (Seddah et al., 2009) have shown that BKY produces *state-of-the-art* performances.

3 French Treebank

For our experiments, we used the French Treebank[4] (Abeillé et al., 2003) [FTB]. It is composed of articles from the newspaper *Le Monde* where each sentence is annotated with a constituent tree. Currently, most of papers about parsing of French use a specific variant of the FTB, namely the FTB-UC described for the first time in (Candito and Crabbé, 2009). It is a partially corrected version of the FTB which contains 12351 sentences and 350931 tokens. This version is smaller[5] and has specific characteristics. First, the tagset takes into account the rich original annotation containing morphological and syntactic information. It results in a tagset of 28 part-of-speech tags. Some compounds with regular syntax schemas are undone into phrases containing simple words. Remaining compounds are merged into a single token, whose components are separated with an underscore.

4 Previous work on word clustering

Numerous works used clustering methods in order to reduce the size of the corpus lexicon and therefore reducing the impact of lexical data sparseness on treebank grammars. A method, described in (Candito and Seddah, 2010) and called *CatLemma*, consists in replacing a word by the combination of its POS tag and its lemma. In the case of a raw text to analyze (notably during evaluations), they used a statistical tagger in order to assign to each word both POS tag and lemma[6].
Instead of reducing each word to the lemmatized form, (Candito and Crabbé, 2009; Candito and Seddah, 2010) have done a morphological clustering, called *desinflection* [DFL], which consists in removing morphological marks that are *less important* for determining syntactic projections in constituents. The mood of verbs is, for example, very helpful. On the other hand, some marks, like gender or number for nouns or the person of verbs, are not so crucial. Moreover, original ambiguities on words are kept in order to delegate the task of POS tags desambiguation to the parser. This algorithm is done with the help of a morpho-syntactic lexicon.
The last clustering method, called *Clust*, consists in replacing each word by a cluster id. Cluster ids are automatically obtained thanks to an unsupervi

[3]The Berkeley Parser is freely available at http ://code.google.com/p/berkeleyparser/

[4]The French Treebank is freely available under licence at http ://www.llf.cnrs.fr/Gens/Abeille/French-Treebank-fr.php

[5]The original FTB contains 20,648 sentences and 580,945 tokens.

[6]They used the tagger MORFETTE (Chrupala et al., 2008; Seddah et al., 2010) which is based on two statistical models, one for tagging and the other for lemmatization. Both models were trained thanks to the *Average Sequence Perceptron* algorithm.

sed statistical algorithm (Brown et al., 1992) applied on a large raw corpus. They are computed by taking account of co-occurrence information of words. The main advantage of this method is the possibility of combining it to *DFL* or *CatLemma*. First, the raw corpus is preprocessed with one of these two methods and then, clusters are computed on this modified corpus. Currently, this method permits to obtain the best results on the FTB-UC.

5 Lexicon-Grammar

The Lexicon-Grammar [LG] is the richest source of syntactic and lexical information for French[7] that focuses not only on verbs but also on verbal nouns, adjectives, adverbs and frozen (or fixed) sentences. Its development started in the 70's by Maurice Gross and his team (Gross, 1994). It is a syntactic lexicon represented in the form of tables. Each table encodes lexical items of a particular category sharing several syntactic properties (e.g. subcategorization information). A lexical item is a lemmatized form which can be present in one or more tables depending on its meaning and its syntactic properties. Each table row corresponds to a lexical item and a column corresponds to a property (e.g. syntactic constructions, argument distribution, and so on). A cell encodes whether a lexical item accepts a given property. Figure 1 shows a sample of verb table *12*. In this table, we can see that the verb *chérir* (*to cherish*) accepts a human subject (pointed out by a + in the property *N0 = : Nhum*) but this verb cannot be intransitive (pointed out by a − in the property *N0 V*). Recently, these tables have been made consistent and explicit (Tolone, 2011) in order to be exploitable for NLP. They also have been transformed in a XML-structured format (Constant and Tolone, 2008)[8]. Each lexical entry is associated with its table identifier, its possible arguments and its syntactic constructions.

For the verbs, we manually constructed a hierarchy of the tables on several levels. Each level contains classes which group LG tables which may not share all their defining properties but have a relatively similar syntactic behavior. Figure 2 shows a sample of the hierarchy. The tables *4, 6* and *12* are grouped into a class called *QTD2* (transitive sentence with two arguments and sentential complements). Then, this class is grouped with other classes at the superior level of the hierarchy to form a class called *TD2* (transitive sentence with two arguments). The characteristics of each level are given in the Table 1 (level 0 represents the set of tables of the LG). We can state that there are 5,923 distinct verbal forms for 13,862 resulting entries in tables of verbs[9]. The column *#classes* specifies the number of distinct classes. The columns *AVG_1* and *AVG_2* respectively indicate the average number of entries per class and the average number of classes per distinct verbal form.

N0 =: Nhum	N0 =: le fait Qu P	N0 =: Vi-inf W	<ENT>Ppv	Ppv =: Neg	<ENT>V	Neg	N0 V	N1 =: Qu Pind	Qu P = V0-inf W	N1 =: Qu P = Aux V0-inf W	N1 = Ppv	[passif par]	[passif de]
+	-	-	<E>	-	chérir	-	-	-	-	-	+	+	+
+	-	-	<E>	-	comprendre	-	+	-	-	-	+	+	+
+	-	-	<E>	-	critiquer	-	+	-	-	-	+	+	+
+	-	-	<E>	-	débiner	-	-	-	-	-	+	+	+

FIG. 1: Sample of verb table *12*.

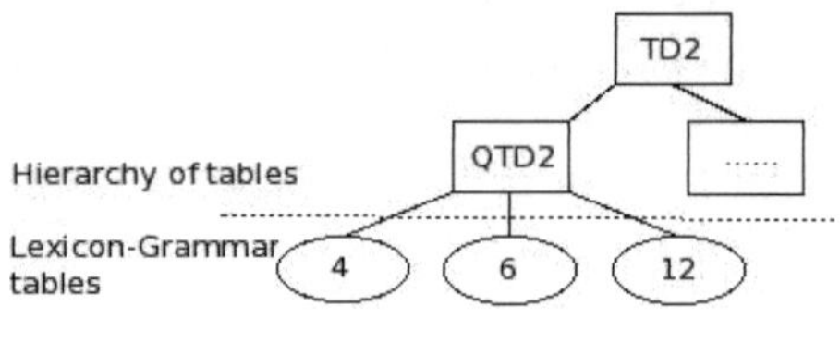

FIG. 2: Sample of the hierarchy of verb tables.

Level	#classes	AVG_1	AVG_2
0	67	207	2.15
1	13	1,066	1.82
2	10	1,386	1.75
3	4	3,465	1.44

TAB. 1: Characteristics of the hierarchy of verb tables.

The hierarchy of tables has the advantage of reducing the number of classes associated with each verb

[7]We can also cite lexicons like LVF (Dubois and Dubois-Charlier, 1997), Dicovalence (Eynde and Piet, 2003) and Lefff (Sagot, 2010).

[8]These resources are freely available at http ://infolingu.univ-mlv.fr/

[9]Note that 3,121 verb forms (3,195 entries) are unambiguous. This means that all their entries occur in a single table.

of the tables. We will see that this ambiguity reduction is crucial in our experiments.

6 Word clustering based on the Lexicon-Grammar

The LG contains a lot of useful information that could be used into the parsing process. But such information is not easily manipulable. We will focus on table identifiers of the verb entries which are important hints about their syntactic behaviors. For example, the table *31R* indicates that all verbs belonging to this table are intransitive. Therefore, we followed the principle of the clustering method *CatLemma*, except that here, we replace each verb of a text by the combination of its POS tag and its table ids associated with this verb in the LG tables[10]. We will call this experiment *TableClust* thereafter. For instance, the verb *chérir* (to cherish) belongs to the table *12*. Therefore, the induced word is *#tag_12*, where *#tag* is the POS tag associated with the verb. For an ambiguous verb like *sanctionner* (to punish), belonging to two tables *6* and *12*, the induced word is *#tag_6_12*.

Then, we have done variants of the previous experiment by taking the hierarchy of verb tables into account. This hierarchy is used to obtain clusters of verbs increasingly coarse as the hierarchy level increases, and at the same time, the size of the corpus lexicon is also increasingly reduced. Identifiers combined to the tag depend on the verb and the specific level in the hierarchy. For example, the verb *sanctionner*, belonging to tables *6* and *12*, is replaced by *#tag_QTD2* at level 1. In the case of ambiguous verbs, for a given level in the hierarchy, identifiers are all classes the verb belongs to. This experiment will be called *LexClust* thereafter.

As for clustering method *CatLemma*, we need a Part-Of-Speech tagger in order to assign a tag and a lemma to each verb of a text (table ids can be determined from the lemma). We made the choice to use *MElt* (Denis and Sagot, 2009) which is one of the best taggers for French. Lemmatization process is done with a French dictionary, the Dela (Courtois and Silberztein, 1990), and some heuristics in the case of ambiguities.

[10]Verbs that are not in the LG remain unchanged.

7 Experiments and results

7.1 Evaluation metrics

As the FTB-UC is a small corpus, we used a *cross-validation* procedure for evaluations. This method consists in splitting the corpus into p equal parts, then we compute training on *p-1* parts and evaluations on the remaining part. We can iterate this process p times. This allows us to calculate an average score for a sample as large as the initial corpus. In our case, we set the parameter p to 10. Results on evaluation parts are reported using the standard protocol called PARSEVAL (Black et al., 1991) for all sentences. The labeled F-Measure [F1] takes into account the bracketing and labeling of nodes. We also use the unlabeled and labeled attachement scores [UAS, LAS] which evaluate the quality of unlabeled and labeled dependencies between words of the sentence[11]. Punctuation tokens are ignored in all metrics.

7.2 Berkeley parser settings

We used a modified version of BKY enhanced for tagging unknown and rare French words (Crabbé and Candito, 2008)[12]. We can notice that BKY uses two sets of sentences at training, a learning set and a validation set for optimizing the grammar parameters. As in (Candito et al., 2010), we used 2% of each training part as a validation set and the remaining 98% as a learning set. The number of split and merge cycles was set to 5.

7.3 Clustering methods

We have evaluated the impact of clustering methods *TableClust* and *LexClust* on the FTB-UC. For both methods, verbal forms of each training part are replaced by the corresponding cluster and, in order to do it on the evaluation part, we use Melt and some heuristics. So as to compare our results with previous work on word clustering, we have reported results of two clustering methods described in section 4, *DFL* and *DFL+Clust* (*Clust* is applied on a text that contains *desinflected* words).

[11]These scores are computed by automatically converting constituent trees into dependency trees. The conversion procedure is made with the *Bonsaï* software, available at http ://alpage.inria.fr/statgram/frdep/fr_stat_dep_parsing.html.

[12]Available in the *Bonsaï* package.

7.4 Evaluations

The experimental results are shown in the Table 2[13]. The column *#lexicon* represents the size of the FTB-UC lexicon according to word clustering methods. In the case of the method *LexClust*, we varied the level of the verbs hierarchy used. The method *TableClust* slightly improves performances compared with the baseline. Nevertheless, using levels of the hierarchy of verb tables through *LexClust* increases results while considerably reducing the size of the corpus lexicon. We obtain the best results with the level 2 of the hierarchy. These performances are almost identical to those of *DFL*, despite the fact that we only modify verbal forms while *DFL* alters all inflected forms regardless of grammatical categories. However, *DFL+Clust* has high scores and is significantly better than *LexClust*. As of this writing, we tried some combination of methods *LexClust* and *Clust* but we observed that both methods are not easily mergeable.

Method	#lexicon	F1	UAS	LAS	F1<40
Baseline	27,143	83.82	89.43	85.85	86.12
DFL	20,127	84.57	89.91	86.36	86.80
DFL+Clust	1,987	85.22	90.26	86.70	87.39
TableClust	24,743	84.11	89.67	86.10	86.53
LexClust 1	22,318	84.33	89.77	86.22	86.62
LexClust 2	21,833	84.44	89.87	86.32	86.76
LexClust 3	20,556	84.26	89.64	86.10	86.57
Tag	20478	84.11	89.58	86.00	86.40
TagLemma	24722	83.87	89.51	85.91	86.26

TAB. 2: Results from cross-validation evaluation according to clustering methods.

The impact of *TableClust* and *LexClust* on a new text is strongly influenced by the quality of the tagging produced by *Melt*. For evaluating this impact, we computed *Gold* experiments for both clustering method. Each verb of evaluation parts, present in the LG tables, is replaced by correct tag and table ids. We observed a gap of almost 0.5% for both tagging and F1. For instance, on the first evaluation part, *Melt* has high but not perfect scores, with a precision of 98.2% and a recall of 97.2%, for a total of 165 errors[14]. About lemmatization, we have a perfect score of 100%.

Our approach is based on the combination of tags and table ids contained in the syntactic lexicon. In order to validate this approach, we have done two other experiments. A first one, called *Tag*, consists in replacing each verbal lemma by its verbal tag only. The second one, called *TagLemma*, consists in the combination of the tag and the lemma. Results are reported in the Table 2. As for *TableClust* and *LexClust*, we replace only verbal forms that are present in the LG tables. We can see that *Tag* has equal performances to *TableClust*. Therefore, original table ids combined with tags are useless. Maybe, the number of clusters is too high and consequently, the size of the corpus lexicon is still too large. However, *LexClust* is better than *Tag*. About *TagLemma*, results are almost identical to the baseline. According to these observations, we can say that verbal clusters created with our method *LexClust* are relevant and useful for a parser like BKY.

We have indicated in Table 3, the top most F1 absolute gains according to phrase labels, for our best clustering method *LexClust* with level 2 of the hierarchy. For each phrase, the column called *Gain* indicates the average F1 absolute gain in comparison to the baseline F1 for this phrase, and *prop.* is the proportion of the phrase in the whole corpus. We can see that three of the five best corrected phrases relate to verbal phrases (plus one if we consider that AdP is linked to a verbal phrase). Therefore, the integration of syntactic data into a clustering algorithm of verbs improves the recognition of verbal phrases.

Phrase label	Meaning	Gain (prop.)
VPpart	participial phrase	4,4% (2%)
Srel	relative clause	1,6% (1%)
VN	verbal nucleus	1.1% (11%)
VPinf	infinitive phrase	0.9% (0.4%)
AdP	adverbial phrase	0.9% (3%)

TAB. 3: Top most F1 absolute gains according to phrases.

8 Conclusion and future work

In this article, we have shown that by using information on verbs from a syntactic lexicon, like the Lexicon-Grammar, we are able to improve performances of a statistical parser based on a PCFG grammar. In the near future, we plan to reproduce experiments with other grammatical categories.

[13] All experiments have a tagging accuracy of about 97%.

[14] We can compute precision and recall scores because sometimes *Melt* wrongly identifies a word as a verb or miss a verb.

References

A. Abeillé, L. Clément, and F. Toussenel. 2003. Building a treebank for French. In Anne Abeillé, editor, *Treebanks : building and using parsed corpora*, Kluwer, Dordrecht.

E. Black, S.Abney, D. Flickinger, C. Gdaniec, R. Grishman, P. Harrison, D. Hindle, R. Ingria, F. Jelinek, J. Klavans, M. Liberman, M. Marcus, S. Roukos, B. Santorini, and T. Strzalkowski. 1991. A procedure for quantitatively comparing the syntactic coverage of english grammars. In *Proceedings of the DARPA Speech and Naturale Language Workshop*, pages 306–311.

T. Briscoe and J. Carroll. 1997. Automatic extraction of subcategorization from corpora. In *Fifth Conference on AppliedNatural Language Processing*, pages 356–363, Washington DC, USA.

P. F. Brown, V. J. Della, P. V. Desouza, J. C. Lai, and R. L. Mercer. 1992. Class-based n-gram models of natural language. In *Computational linguistics, 18(4)*, pages 467–479.

M. Candito and B. Crabbé. 2009. Improving generative statistical parsing with semi-supervised word clustering. In *Proceedings of the 11th International Conference on Parsing Technology (IWPT'09)*, pages 138–141.

M. Candito and D. Seddah. 2010. Parsing word clusters. In *Proceedings of the first NAACL HLT Workshop on Morphologically-Rich Languages (SPRML2010)*, pages 76–84, Los Angeles, California.

M. Candito, B. Crabbé, and P. Denis. 2010. Statistical French dependency parsing : treebank conversion and first results. In *Proceedings of LREC10*.

J. Carroll and A. C. Fang. 2004. The automatic acquisition of verb subcategorisations and their impact on the performance of an HPSG parser. In *Proceedings of the 1st International Conference onNatural Language Processing*, Sanya City, China.

G. Chrupala, G. Dinu, and J. van Genabith. 2008. Learning morphology with Morfette. In *Proceedings of LREC 2008*.

M. Constant and E. Tolone. 2008. A generic tool to generate a lexicon for nlp from lexicon-grammar tables. In *Actes du 27ème Colloque Lexique et Grammaire*, L'Aquila, Italie.

B. Courtois and M. Silberztein. 1990. Dictionnaires électroniques du français. Présentation. In *Larousse, editor, Langue Française*.

B. Crabbé and M. Candito. 2008. Expériences d'analyse syntaxique statistique du français. In *Actes de la 15ème Conférence sur le Traitement Automatique des Langues Naturelles (TALN'08)*, pages 45–54, Avignon, France.

P. Denis and B. Sagot. 2009. Coupling an annotated corpus and a morphosyntactic lexicon for state-of-the-art pos tagging with less human effort. In *PACLIC 2009*, Hong Kong.

T. Deoskar. 2008. Re-estimation of lexical parameters for treebank PCFGs. In *Proceedings of the 22nd International Conference on Computational Linguistics (Coling 2008)*, pages 193–200, Manchester, Great Britain.

J. Dubois and F. Dubois-Charlier. 1997. *Les verbes français*. Larousse-Bordas.

K. Eynde and M. Piet. 2003. La valence : l'approche pronominale et son application au lexique verbal. *Journal of French Language studies*, pages 63–104.

M. Gross. 1994. Constructing Lexicon-grammars. In Atkins and Zampolli, editors, *Computational Approaches to the Lexicon*, pages 213–263.

T. Koo, X. Carreras, and M. Collins. 2008. Simple semi-supervised dependency parsing. In *Proceedings of ACL-08*.

T. Matsuzaki, Y. Miyao, and J. Tsujii. 2005. Probabilistic CFG with latent annotations. In *Proceedings of ACL-05*, pages 75–82, Ann Arbor, USA.

R. O'Donovan, A. Cahill, A. Way, M. Burke, and J. van Genabith. 2005. Large-Scale induction and evaluation of lexical resources from the Penn-II and Penn-III Treebanks. In *Computational Linguistics, 31*, pages 329–366.

S. Petrov, L. Barrett, R. Thibaux, and D. Klein. 2006. Learning accurate, compact, and interpretable tree annotation. In *Proceedings of the 21st International Conference on Computational Linguistics and 44th Annual Meeting of the Association for Computational Linguistics*, Sydney, Australia.

B. Sagot. 2010. The Lefff, a freely available, accurate and large-coverage lexicon for French. In *Proceedings of LREC 2010*, La Valette, Malte.

N. Schluter and J. Van Genabith. 2008. Treebank-Based Acquisition of LFG Parsing Resources for French. In *Proceedings of LREC08*, Marrakech, Morocco.

D. Seddah, M. Candito, and B. Crabbé. 2009. Adaptation de parsers statistiques lexicalisés pour le français : Une évaluation complète sur corpus arborés. In *Actes de la 15ème Conférence sur le Traitement Automatique des Langues Naturelles (TALN'09)*, Senlis, France.

D. Seddah, G. Chrupala, O. Cetinoglu, J. van Genabith, and M. Candito. 2010. Lemmatization and statistical lexicalized parsing of morphologically-rich languages. In *Proceedings of the first NAACL HLT Workshop on Morphologically-Rich Languages (SPRML2010)*.

E. Tolone. 2011. *Analyse syntaxique à l'aide des tables du Lexique-Grammaire du français*. Ph.D. thesis, Université Paris-Est Marne-la-Vallée.

Testing the Effect of Morphological Disambiguation in Dependency Parsing of Basque

Kepa Bengoetxea, Koldo Gojenola
IXA NLP Group
University of the Basque Country
Technical School of Engineering, Bilbao
{kepa.bengoetxea, koldo.gojenola}@ehu.es

Arantza Casillas
IXA NLP Group
University of the Basque Country
Faculty of Science and Technology
arantza.casillas@ehu.es

Abstract

This paper presents a set of experiments performed on parsing Basque, a morphologically rich and agglutinative language, studying the effect of using the morphological analyzer for Basque together with the morphological disambiguation module, in contrast to using the gold standard tags taken from the treebank. The objective is to obtain a first estimate of the effect of errors in morphological analysis and disambiguation on the parsers. We tested two freely available and state of the art dependency parser generators, MaltParser, and MST, which represent the two dominant approaches in data-driven dependency parsing.

1 Introduction

There have been lots of attempts at parsing the Basque Dependency Treebank (BDT, Aduriz et al. 2003), starting from the CoNLL 2007 Shared Task on Dependency Parsing (Nivre et al. 2007a), where multiple systems competed on getting the best parsing results, and continued by the work done by Bengoetxea and Gojenola (2009a, 2009b, 2010). However, in all of these works, the input to the parser was the set of gold standard part of speech (POS) and morphosyntactic tags (corresponding to case, number and a number of morphological information types) taken directly from the treebank, meaning that there were no errors in the first stage of converting raw texts to morphosyntactically analyzed ones, previous to applying the parsers.

Typically, morphologically rich languages are morphologically very ambiguous. For example, in the case of Basque, each word can receive multiple affixes, as each lemma can generate thousands of word-forms by means of morphological properties, such as case, number, tense, or different types of subordination for verbs. Consequently, the morphological analyzer for Basque (Aduriz et al. 2000) gives a high ambiguity. If only categorial (POS) ambiguity is taken into account, there is an average of 1.55 interpretations per word-form, which rises to 2.65 when the full morphosyntactic information is taken into account, giving an overall 64% of ambiguous word-forms. Disambiguating the output of morphological analysis, in order to obtain a single interpretation for each word-form, can pose an important problem, as determining the correct interpretation for each word-form requires in many cases the inspection of local contexts, and in some others, as the agreement of verbs with subject, object or indirect object, it could also suppose the examination of elements which can be far from each other, added to the free constituent order of the main sentence elements in Basque. The erroneous assignment of incorrect interpretations, regarding to part of speech or to morphological features, can difficult the work of the parser.

For that reason, in this work we have attempted the first evaluation of two data-driven parser generators, taking the output of the morphological analysis and disambiguation as their input. As morphological ambiguity is very high compared to other languages such as English, this could hypothetically harm the results of syntactic analyzers.

Although there have been several attempts at integrating morphological and syntactic processing of several languages such as Hebrew (Goldberg and Tsarfaty 2008) or Latin, Czech, Greek and Hungarian (Lee et al. 2011), in the present work we will test the simpler option of using a pipelined approach, where the texts are passed first through morphosyntactic analysis and disambiguation, forcing a single interpretation per word-form, and then passing it to the parser. This can give an upper limit on the increase of the error rate due to incorrect interpretations from morphological disam-

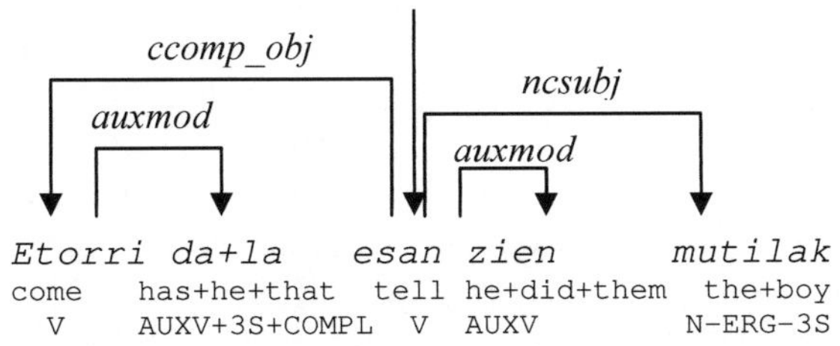

Figure 1. Dependency tree for the sentence *Etorri dela esan zien mutilak.*
(V = main verb, N = noun, AUXV = auxiliary verb, COMPL = completive, ccomp_obj = clausal complement object, ERG = ergative, S: singular, auxmod = auxiliary, ncsubj = non-clausal subject).

biguation, and could also serve as a starting point for more elaborate integrated approximations.

2 Resources

This section will describe the main resources that have been used in the experiments. First, subsection 2.1 will describe the Basque Dependency Treebank (BDT), subsection 2.2 will explain the main details of the morphological analysis and disambiguation modules for Basque (Aduriz et al. 1997, 2000), while subsection 2.3 will present the main characteristics of MaltParser, and MST, two state of the art data-driven dependency parsers.

2.1 The Basque Dependency Treebank

Basque can be described as an agglutinative language that presents a high power to generate inflected word-forms, with free constituent order of sentence elements with respect to the main verb. The BDT can be considered a pure dependency treebank from its original design, due mainly to the syntactic characteristics of Basque.

```
Etorri  dela    esan  zien  mutilak
come   that-has tell  did   boy-the
The boy told them that he had come
```

Example 1. Example of a treebank sentence.

Figure 1 presents the sentence from example 1. Each word contains its form, lemma, category (POS), subcategory, morphological features, and the dependency relation (headword + dependency). The information in Figure 1 has been simplified due to space reasons, as typically each word contains many *morphosyntactic*[1] features (case, number, type of subordinated sentence, …), which are relevant for parsing. The first version of the Basque Dependency Treebank contained 55,469 tokens forming 3,700 sentences (Aduriz et al., 2003), and it was used as one of the evaluated treebanks in the CoNLL 2007 Shared Task on Dependency Parsing (Nivre et al., 2007a). Our work will make use of the second version of the BDT, which is the result of a extension and redesign of the original requirements, containing 150,000 tokens (11,225 sentences), a three-fold increase.

2.2 Morphological Analysis

The morphological analyzer for Basque (Aduriz et al. 2000) consists of two subsystems. The first one performs a robust analysis based on two-level morphology, while the second part organizes the rich information contained in each word-form, by means of a unification-based grammar. This word-level grammar organizes the wealth of information provided by suffixes corresponding to derivation, word composition, and affixes that convey information about case or number (nouns, adjectives, determiners but also verbs), aspect, tense and morphemes corresponding to different types of subordination (for verbal categories).

The output of the morphological analyzer contains 2.65 interpretations per word-form. For example, the verb *zien* in figure 1 is ambiguous between a main verb and an auxiliary, and each interpretation is also ambiguous, as it can be a past tense verb, a relative sentence or an indirect interrogative question, giving 6 interpretations.

Next, there is a module for morphological disambiguation (Ezeiza et al. 1998), which uses a combination of knowledge-based disambiguation, by means of the Constraint Grammar formalism (Karlsson et al. 1995, Aduriz et al. 1997), and a posterior statistical disambiguation module, using an HMM. This second statistical module can be parameterized according to the level of disambiguation that the user wants to obtain, in an attempt to trade off precision and recall. For example, the system allows to only disambiguate based on the main categories, abstracting over

[1] We will use the term *morphosyntactic* to name the set of features attached to each word-form, which by the agglutinative nature of Basque correspond to both morphology and syntax.

morphosyntactic features. This option maintains most of the correct interpretations but, on the other hand, it still gives an output with several interpretations per word-form (for example, the system chooses the correct category, but does not decide on case or number ambiguity). In our experiments we applied the option that disambiguated most. This option maintains more than 97% of the correct interpretations, still leaving a remaining ambiguity of 1.3 interpretations, that can be considered high compared to languages like English. The 97% limit was established as a compromise between recall and precision, as in Karlsson et al. (1995).

2.3 Parsers

We have made use of MaltParser (Nivre et al. 2007b, Nivre 2006) and MSTParser (McDonald et al. 2006), two state of the art dependency parsers representing two dominant approaches in data-driven dependency parsing, and that have been successfully applied to typologically different languages and treebanks (McDonald and Nivre 2007).

MaltParser is a representative of local, greedy, transition-based dependency parsing models, where the parser obtains deterministically a dependency tree in a single pass over the input using two data structures: a stack of partially analyzed items and the remaining input sequence. To determine the best action at each step, the parser uses history-based feature models and discriminative machine learning. The specification of the learning configuration can include any kind of information (such as word-form, lemma, category, subcategory or morphological features). Several variants of the parser have been implemented, and we will use one of its standard versions (MaltParser version 1.4). In our experiments, we will use the Stack-Lazy algorithm with the *liblinear* classifier.

MSTParser can be considered a representative of global, exhaustive graph-based parsing (McDonald et al. 2005, 2006). This algorithm finds the highest scoring directed spanning tree in a dependency graph forming a valid dependency tree. To learn arc scores, it uses large-margin structured learning algorithms, which optimize the parameters of the model to maximize the score margin between the correct dependency graph and all incorrect dependency graphs for every sentence in a training set. The learning procedure is global since model parameters are set relative to classifying the entire dependency graph, and not just over single arc attachments. This is in contrast to the local but richer contexts used by transition-based parsers.

We use the freely available version of MSTParser[2]. In the experiments we will make use of the second order non-projective algorithm, which gave the better results on the base treebank.

3 Experiments and Evaluation

In this section we will first present the process of annotating the treebank with the tags given by morphological analysis and disambiguation, and then we will report the main results.

3.1 Morphological Analysis / Disambiguation

When applying morphological analysis and disambiguation to a treebank that was manually annotated, there is the problem of matching the tokens of the treebank with those obtained from the morphological analyzer, as there were divergences on the treatment of multiword units, mostly coming from Named Entities, verb compounds and complex postpositions (those formed with morphemes appearing at two different words). For that reason, we performed a matching process trying to link the multiword units given by the morphological analysis module and those of the treebank, obtaining a correct match for about two thirds of the multiwords. Named Entities had the best matching score, while other phenomena such as complex postpositions, which have a wide variety, were not covered at all. After this matching stage, we selected those sentences giving a one-to-one direct correspondence for each token. This left us with a considerable reduction of the data, from the original 150,000 tokens to 97,000. The alignment of the rest of the sentences is left as future work. The reduction on the treebank size could lead to question about the relevance of the remaining data after the non-matching sentences have been discarded, because it could seem that those sentences were harder to parse (in principle they are candidates to having more morphological errors). However, the results on the full and the reduced treebanks confirmed that the reduction in accuracy was proportional to the treebank size, meaning that discarding a portion of the treebank did not have any side effects apart from a proportional drop in the results.

[2] http://mstparser.sourceforge.net

	MaltParser		MSTParser	
	LAS	UAS	LAS	UAS
Baseline (training = gold tags, test = gold tags)	78.78%	84.02%	78.93%	84.94%
Training = gold tags, test = automatic tags	76.57% (-2.21)	82.24% (-1.78)	76.62% (-2.31)	82.91% (-2.03)
Training = automatic tags, test = automatic tags	76.77% (-2.01)	82.46% (-1.56)	77.20% (-1.73)	83.76% (-1.18)

Table 1. Evaluation results.
(LAS: Labeled Attachment Score, UAS: Unlabeled Attachment Score)

As the morphological disambiguation process leaves a reduced ambiguity of 1.3 interpretations per word-form, and the parsers we will use require a single interpretation, we took the simplest option of choosing the first interpretation, which corresponds to taking the most frequent option. This leaves open the investigation of more complex approaches trying to select the most appropriate reading. This is not an easy task, as the ambiguity left is the hardest to solve, because the knowledge-based and statistical disambiguation processes have not been able to determine a single reading. Among the remaining types of ambiguity that were left, we can distinguish several types:

- Nominal. It includes all the categories that can bear case, such as nouns, adjectives and determiners (but also verbs). The *case* feature is important, as it carries the information necessary to correctly attach NPs and postpositional phrases to main verbs. It appears only at the last noun of the whole phrase.
- Verbal. Auxiliary verbs are very ambiguous, as all of them can also be interpreted as main verbs. Moreover, all of the past tense verbs are additionally ambiguous regarding several types of subordination sentences (relative clause, indirect interrogative or modal).

3.2 Results

Table 1 shows the results of applying the two parsers on the selected data. We did the typical train-development-test split, using 80%, 10% and 10% of the test data, respectively. In the present work we only performed a single run for each experiment, so we did not made use of the development set, using directly the test set for evaluation. For future work, we plan to use the development set for experimenting different alternatives. The first line in table 1 shows the baseline when using the gold standard tags, in accord with previous results on parsing the BDT (Bengoetxea and Gojenola 2010).

For testing the output of automatic morphological processing we performed two different kinds of experiment. In the first set we used the treebank with the gold standard tags for training. In the second option we trained the parsers giving as input the training set with the tags obtained after the process of morphological disambiguation. This way, the parsers were trained on the output from morphological disambiguation, and we will be able to compare whether it is better to train the parser using gold morphological tags or otherwise the parsers can benefit learning from the real input using morphological analysis and disambiguation.

The second line in table 1 shows that, when using the gold standard tags from the treebank for training, both parsers suffer a similar decrease in accuracy in LAS and UAS of approximately two absolute points, which is surprising in our opinion, as we expected a bigger drop in performance due to the potentially hard task of reducing 2.65 interpretations per word-form to a single interpretation. This can be due in part to the careful approach to disambiguation, combining both rule-based and statistical disambiguation (Ezeiza et al. 1998), but we must also acknowledge the use of a very robust tool for morphological analysis (Aduriz et al. 2000), which reduces the number of unrecognized or incorrectly analyzed words, incorporating sophisticated algorithms for handling out of vocabulary words, e.g. special types of two-level rules for them. On the other hand, we can also say that some morphosyntactic errors can be transparent to the parsers, as some categorial errors, e.g. noun versus adjective, will not harm the parser as long as the morphological information (basically case) is correct, because the correct determination of the case is what the parser needs to assign the correct dependency relation (subject, object or modifier).

The table also shows (third line) that the results improve when training the parsers with the same tags provided by automatic morphological analysis and disambiguation, as the parsers can in some

	MaltParser	MSTParser
	LAS	LAS
Baseline (training and test with gold tags)	78.78%	78.93%
Training = automatic tags, test = automatic tags	76.77%	77.20%
Sentences with errors in morphological tags (correct POS)	75.48%	75.96%
Sentences with errors in POS tags	72.13%	72.21%

Table 2. Evaluation results on sentences with morphosyntactic errors.

way *learn* working on the errors of the morphological modules. We also see that MSTParser seems to be slightly more robust than MaltParser when dealing with automatically obtained morphosyntactic tags, although not statistically significant.

In order to have a more detailed snapshot of the decrease of performance, we selected two subsets of sentences for a more detailed evaluation, with the aim of examining the effect of morphological disambiguation, counting only the sentences containing disambiguation errors. This will allow a better estimate of the impact of errors on these sentences. We distinguished two types of errors:

- Errors in POS. In principle, these errors could be considered the most harmful, as an error determining the main category of a word can have devastating effects. For example, this errors can typically result from the confusion of a verb as a noun or adjective. Another important subtype of this set of errors is the distinction between main and auxiliary verbs.
- Errors in morphosyntactic features (with the correct POS). They can also have an important impact on the results. For example, there is a systematic ambiguity between the ergative and the absolutive cases, which is closely related to determining the subject and object of a sentence. Another type corresponds to past tense verbs, which are ambiguous between a simple past tense verb, a relative sentence or an indirect interrogative sentence.

Table 2 shows how the performance drops around three absolute points with respect to the gold standard tags when we only take the sentences containing morphosyntactic errors (around half of the sentences), and six points when considering sentences with categorial or POS errors (which affects to one quarter of the sentences).

4 Conclusions and future work

We have presented a set of experiments studying the effect of using the morphological analyzer for Basque, in contrast to using the gold standard tags taken from the treebank. The objective was to obtain a first estimate of the effect of errors in morphological analysis and disambiguation on the parsers. We tested two different freely available and state of the art dependency parser generators, MaltParser and MSTParser.

As a main result, we can say that the errors due to incorrect disambiguation are not as important as it could be initially expected due to the high morphosyntactic ambiguity given by the Basque morphological analyzer. We have shown how morphological disambiguation errors drop the performance of the parsers in 2 absolute LAS points. MSTParser seems to be slightly more robust than MaltParser, although by a small difference.

For a future work we leave the task of correctly disambiguating the ambiguous sets of morphosyntactic readings. This could be solved by either integrating parsing and disambiguation (Cohen and Smith 2007, Goldberg and Tsarfaty 2008, Lee et al. 2011) or also redesigning the currently used modules. The key could be that the morphological disambiguation module that we used was defined independently, trying to maximize the number of correctly disambiguated tokens, while the same system could also be optimized having parsing in mind, that is, examining which kind of disambiguation errors give the most/less parsing errors. Another important line of research consists in a careful examination of the errors regarding to different types of part of speech and dependency relations, which can provide new insights.

Acknowledgements

This research was supported by the Department of Industry of the Basque Government (IE09-262, IT344-10), the University of the Basque Country (GIU09/19, INF10/65) and the Spanish Ministry of Science and Innovation (MICINN, TIN2010-20218, TIN2009-06135-E, TEC2009-06876-E/TEC, TIN2009-14675-C03-01).

References

Aduriz I., Arriola J.M., Artola X., Díaz de Ilarraza A., Gojenola K., Maritxalar M. 1997. Morphosyntactic disambiguation for Basque based on the Constraint Grammar Formalism. Conference on *Recent Advances in Natural Language Processing* (RANLP), Bulgaria.

Itziar Aduriz, Eneko Agirre, Izaskun Aldezabal, Iñaki Alegria, Xabier Arregi, Jose Mari Arriola, Xabier Artola, Koldo Gojenola, Montserrat Maritxalar, Kepa Sarasola, and Miriam Urkia. 2000. A word-grammar based morphological analyzer for agglutinative languages. *Coling 2000*, Saarbrucken.

Itziar Aduriz, Maria Jesus Aranzabe, Jose Maria Arriola, Aitziber Atutxa, Arantza Diaz de Ilarraza, Aitzpea Garmendia and Maite Oronoz. 2003. Construction of a Basque dependency treebank. *Treebanks and Linguistic Theories*.

Xabier Artola, Arantza Díaz de Ilarraza, Nerea Ezeiza, Koldo Gojenola, Gorka Labaka, Aitor Sologaistoa, Aitor Soroa. 2005. A framework for representing and managing linguistic annotations based on typed feature structures. *Proceedings of the International Conference on Recent Advances in Natural Language Processing*, RANLP 2005.

Kepa Bengoetxea and Koldo Gojenola. 2009a. Exploring Treebank Transformations in Dependency Parsing. *Proceedings of the International Conference on Recent Advances in Natural Language Processing*, RANLP'2009.

Kepa Bengoetxea and Koldo Gojenola. 2009b. Application of feature propagation to dependency parsing. *Proceedings of the International Workshop on Parsing Technologies* (IWPT'2009).

Kepa Bengoetxea and Koldo Gojenola. 2010. Application of Different Techniques to Dependency Parsing of Basque. Proceedings of *the 1st Workshop on Statistical Parsing of Morphologically Rich Languages* (SPMRL), NAACL-HLT Workshop, Los Angeles, USA.

Shay B. Cohen and Noah A. Smith. 2007. Joint Morphological and Syntactic Disambiguation. *In Proceedings of the CoNLL 2007 Shared Task.*

Gülsen Eryiğit, Joakim Nivre and Kemal Oflazer. 2008. Dependency Parsing of Turkish. *Computational Linguistics*, Vol. 34 (3).

Ezeiza N., Alegria I., Arriola J.M., Urizar R., Aduriz I. 1998. Combining Stochastic and Rule-Based Methods for Disambiguation in Agglutinative Languages. *COLING-ACL'98*, Montreal.

Yoav Goldberg and Reut Tsarfaty. 2008. A Single Generative Model for Joint Morphological Segmentation and Syntactic Parsing. *Proceedings of ACL-HLT* 2008, Colombus, Ohio, USA.

Karlsson F., Voutilainen A., Heikkila J., Anttila A. 1995. *Constraint Grammar: A Language-independent System for Parsing Unrestricted Text.* Mouton de Gruyter.

John Lee, Jason Naradowsky and David A. Smith. 2011. A Discriminative Model for Joint Morphological Disambiguation and Dependency Parsing. ACL-HLT 2011, Portland, USA.

R. McDonald, K. Crammer, and F. Pereira. 2005. Online large-margin training of dependency parsers. In Proc. ACL.

R. McDonald, K. Lerman, and F. Pereira. 2006. Multilingual dependency analysis with a two-stage discriminative parser. In Proc. CoNLL.

Ryan McDonald and Joakim Nivre. 2007. Characterizing the Errors of Data-Driven Dependency Parsing Models. Proceedings of the 2007 *Joint Conference on Empirical Methods in Natural Language Processing and Computational Natural Language Learning*, EMNLP/CoNLL, Prague.

Joakim Nivre. 2006. *Inductive Dependency Parsing.* Springer.

Joakim Nivre, Johan Hall, Sandra Kübler, Ryan McDonald, Jens Nilsson, Sebastian Riedel and Deniz Yuret. 2007a. The CoNLL 2007 Shared Task on Dependency Parsing. *Proceedings of EMNLP-CoNLL.*

Joakim Nivre, Johan Hall, Jens Nilsson, Chanev A., Gülsen Eryiğit, Sandra Kübler, Marinov S., and Edwin Marsi. 2007b. MaltParser: A language-independent system for data-driven dependency parsing. *Natural Language Engineering.*

Joakim Nivre and Ryan McDonald. 2008. Integrating graph-based and transition-based dependency parsers. *Proceedings* of ACL-2008.

Discontinuous Data-Oriented Parsing: A mildly context-sensitive all-fragments grammar

Andreas van Cranenburgh, Remko Scha, and Federico Sangati
Institute for Logic, Language and Computation
University of Amsterdam
Science Park 904, 1098 XH Amsterdam, The Netherlands
acranenb@science.uva.nl, scha@uva.nl, f.sangati@uva.nl

Abstract

Recent advances in parsing technology have made treebank parsing with discontinuous constituents possible, with parser output of competitive quality (Kallmeyer and Maier, 2010). We apply Data-Oriented Parsing (DOP) to a grammar formalism that allows for discontinuous trees (LCFRS). Decisions during parsing are conditioned on all possible fragments, resulting in improved performance. Despite the fact that both DOP and discontinuity present formidable challenges in terms of computational complexity, the model is reasonably efficient, and surpasses the state of the art in discontinuous parsing.

1 Introduction

Many natural language phenomena are inherently not context-free, or call for structural descriptions that cannot be produced by a context-free grammar (Chomsky, 1957; Shieber, 1985; Savitch et al., 1987). Examples are extraposition, cross-serial dependencies and WH-inversion. However, relaxing the context-freeness assumption comes at the peril of combinatorial explosion.

This work aims to transcend two limitations associated with probabilistic context-free grammars. First in the sense of the representations produced by the parser, which allow constituents with gaps in their yields (see figure 1). Building on Kallmeyer and Maier (2010), we parse with a mildly context-sensitive grammar (LCFRS) that can be read off directly from a treebank annotated with discontinuous constituents.

Secondly, the statistical dependencies in our generative model are derived from arbitrarily large fragments from the corpus. We employ a Data-Oriented Parsing (DOP) model: a probabilistic tree-substitution grammar that employs probabilities derived from the frequencies of all connected fragments in the treebank (Bod, 1992; Bansal and Klein, 2010; Sangati and Zuidema, 2011). We generalize the DOP model to support discontinuity. This allows us to model complex constructions such as *NP kann man VVINF*.

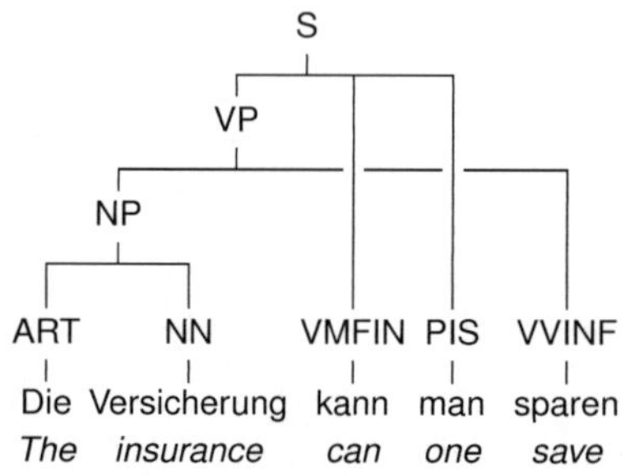

Figure 1: A discontinuous tree from the Negra corpus. Translation: *As for the insurance, one can save it.*

2 Motivation

Treebank grammars need not be mere exercises in machine learning; they may be significant steps toward cognitively viable models of human language processing. To develop the enterprise of corpus-based parsing in this more ambitious direction, substantial questions must be faced—methodological as well as technical ones.

All successful treebank grammars now employ very large numbers of rules; these rules, extracted from the corpus, are extremely specific and could never be motivated by abstract linguistic considerations. They either use large and complex fragments of the corpus trees (the Data-Oriented

Parsing approach), or they introduce specialized non-terminal labels which encode non-local information about the occurrence contexts of the nodes (the symbol-refinement approach). (These two methods are in fact not unrelated, as we shall discuss below.) Both approaches use "grammars" in the technical sense (bodies of rewrite rules), but not in the linguistic sense. The grammars do not encode general properties of the language, but specific properties of the corpus. All interesting treebank grammars are thus essentially exemplar-based. This characterization applies even more unavoidably to discriminative models that use the corpus trees directly without any kind of intervening grammar.

The exemplar-based models implemented by modern statistical parsers are of potential interest to the theory of language cognition, because they are the first formal alternatives to the rule-based models espoused by modern linguistics. But the tests that drive the development of statistical parsers are not sufficient to establish their plausibility as cognitive models. For corpus-based language processing work to become more relevant to language cognition, innovations are needed along several dimensions. One of them is evaluation methodology. F_1-scores on labeled bracketings constitute a poor criterion of excellence. More qualitative analyses are needed; we must try to understand what works and what doesn't.

In the present paper we do not deal with evaluation methods, but we take up another, related point. A precondition for a cognitively viable model of exemplar-based syntactic processing, is a cognitively viable definition of "syntactic Gestalts," i.e., of the kinds of objects that occur in the corpus and that are to be produced by the parser. It is customary to employ "syntactic surface trees" for this purpose, i.e., labeled trees with ordered branches, having the words of the sentence as their leaves. When we look at languages with a relatively free word order (which often correlates with a relatively non-trivial morphology), limitations of this approach become apparent. In such languages, the intuitive "parts" of the sentence need not coincide with contiguous surface constituents. By introducing movement features and allowing empty constituents, it is possible to encode non-local connections inside ordered surface trees; at the same time, functional feature labels may be added to the surface-syntactic categories. This approach was taken in the Penn Treebank (Taylor et al., 2003). In principle, this makes it possible to extract functional structures from the corpus-trees, and also, to evaluate parsers on their capacity to correctly construct the functional structures of test sentences. In practice, however, this is hardly ever done.

In English, the discrepancies between functional structure and surface constituents are less prominent than in many other languages. It is no coincidence that this issue was first squarely faced by the designers of the annotation conventions of the German Negra and Tiger corpora (Skut et al., 1997; Brants et al., 2002). They chose to use unordered trees (with crossing branches), allowing discontinuous constituents that correspond directly to the intuitively perceived argument structures. A model using a corpus annotated in this way, would be more interesting from a cognitive point of view, because it employs more plausible exemplars, and its output can be compared with more meaningful "gold trees."

Much of the work that used the Tiger and Negra corpora has failed to take advantage of this situation. Typically, these corpora are converted into traditional phrase-structure trees, so as to allow the application of the standard American techniques that were developed for English corpora. Exceptions were Plaehn (2004) and Maier (2010). The current paper follows up on that work, and integrates it with the Data-Oriented Parsing approach.

3 Discontinuity

Our symbolic grammar is a Linear Context-Free Rewriting System (Vijay-Shanker et al., 1987). LCFRS was introduced to subsume a wide variety of mildly context-sensitive formalisms (e.g., TAG, CCG, and even synchronous CFG). Intuitively it can be seen as a generalization of context-free grammar to other structures: rules are context-free, but instead of strings they rewrite tuples, trees or graphs. In our case a non-terminal may cover a tuple of discontinuous strings instead of a single, contiguous sequence of terminals. The number of components in such a tuple is called the *fan-out* of a rule, which is equal to the number of gaps plus one; the fan-out of the grammar is the maximum fan-out of its rules. A context-free grammar is a LCFRS with a fan-out of 1. For convenience we will will use the rule notation of simple RCG (Boullier, 1998), which is a syntactic variant of LCFRS.

A LCFRS is a tuple $G = \langle N, T, V, P, S \rangle$. N is a finite set of non-terminals; a function $dim : N \rightarrow \mathbb{N}$ specifies the unique fan-out for every non-terminal symbol. T and V are disjoint finite sets of terminals and variables. S is the distinguished start symbol with $dim(S) = 1$. P is a finite set of rewrite rules of the form:

$$A(\alpha_1, \ldots \alpha_{dim(A)}) \rightarrow B_1(X_1^1, \ldots, X_{dim(B_1)}^1) \ldots B_m(X_1^m, \ldots, X_{dim(B_m)}^m)$$

for $m \geq 0$, where $A, B_1, \ldots, B_m \in N$, each $X_j^i \in V$ for $1 \leq i \leq m, 1 \leq j \leq dim(A_j)$ and $\alpha_i \in (T \cup V)^*$ for $1 \leq i \leq dim(A_i)$.

Rules must be *linear*: if a variable occurs in a rule, it occurs exactly once on the left hand side (LHS), and exactly once on the right hand side (RHS). A rule is *ordered* if for any two variables X_1 and X_2 occurring in a non-terminal on the RHS, X_1 precedes X_2 on the LHS iff X_1 precedes X_2 on the RHS.

A rule can be *instantiated* when its variables can be bound to spans such that for each component α_i of the LHS, the concatenation of its terminals and bound variables forms a contiguous span in the input, while the endpoints of each span are non-contiguous.

As in the case of a PCFG, we can read off LCFRS rules from a treebank (Maier and Søgaard, 2008), and the relative frequencies of rules form a maximum likelihood estimate, for a probabilistic LCFRS (PLCFRS). The tree in figure 1 decomposes into the following productions:

$$\begin{aligned}
&\mathrm{S}(x_0x_1x_2x_3) &&\rightarrow \mathrm{VP}_2(x_0, x_3)\ \mathrm{VMFIN}(x_1)\ \mathrm{PIS}(x_2)\\
&\mathrm{VP}_2(x_0, x_1) &&\rightarrow \mathrm{NP}(x_0)\ \mathrm{VVINF}(x_1)\\
&\mathrm{NP}(x_0x_1) &&\rightarrow \mathrm{ART}(x_0)\ \mathrm{NN}(x_1)\\
&\mathrm{ART}(\mathrm{Die}) &&\rightarrow \varepsilon\\
&\mathrm{NN}(\mathrm{Versicherung}) &&\rightarrow \varepsilon\\
&\mathrm{VVINF}(\mathrm{sparen}) &&\rightarrow \varepsilon\\
&\mathrm{VMFIN}(\mathrm{kann}) &&\rightarrow \varepsilon\\
&\mathrm{PIS}(\mathrm{man}) &&\rightarrow \varepsilon
\end{aligned}$$

Discontinuous non-terminals are annotated with a number indicating their fan-out, to satisfy the restriction that each non-terminal type A can be mapped to a unique fan-out by $dim(A)$. A derivation proceeds by instantiating rules with subsequences of terminals in the input. Each non-terminal can be seen as a predicate holding over part of the sentence. Following the framework of deductive parsing (Nederhof, 2003), a sentence is parsed in a sequence of weighted deduction steps aiming at the goal theorem, viz., the start symbol covering the whole input in a single span.

Algorithm 1 A probabilistic agenda-based CKY parser for LCFRS.

initialize agenda $\mathcal{A}$ with POS tags
`while` $\mathcal{A} \neq \emptyset$
  $\langle I, x \rangle \leftarrow$ item with lowest score on agenda
  add $\langle I, x \rangle$ to $\mathcal{C}$ and $\mathcal{F}$
  `for all` $\langle I', y \rangle$ deduced from $\{\langle I, J \rangle, \langle J, I \rangle, \langle I \rangle \mid J \in \mathcal{C}\}$
    `if` $I' \notin \mathcal{A} \cup \mathcal{C}$
      enqueue $\langle I', y \rangle$ in $\mathcal{A}$
    `else if` $I' \in \mathcal{A} \wedge y <$ score for I' in $\mathcal{A}$
      add I' with old score to $\mathcal{F}$
      update weight of I' in $\mathcal{A}$ to y
    `else`
      add $\langle I', y \rangle$ to $\mathcal{F}$

This work employs an extended version of the agenda-based CKY parser for LCFRS in Kallmeyer and Maier (2010). The algorithm is Knuth's generalization of Dijkstra's shortest path algorithm to the case of hypergraphs, where the shortest path is the Viterbi derivation and the hypergraph is the chart defining possible derivations. A requirement of a CKY parser is that rules are binarized; we also restrict the parser to ordered rules for efficiency. The search space of a PCFG can be explored systematically from left to right with constituents of increasing size; this is what makes typical CKY parsers efficient. Unfortunately this approach does not translate to LCFRS because discontinuous constituents can cover any subsequence of the input. For this reason an explicit agenda has to be used, which we order by inside probability; alternatively the agenda can employ figures of merit or A* heuristics, but this is not explored in this work.

Our implementation[1] produces an exhaustive chart instead of stopping at the Viterbi derivation. The pseudo-code is given in algorithm 1. The

[1]The parser including source code is publicly available from `http://github.com/andreasvc/disco-dop`. Everything was written in Python, with pre-processing and evaluation making use of NLTK (Bird et al., 2009), and the parser and k-best extraction making use of Cython (Behnel et al., 2011) to translate Python code with static type annotations to native C code.

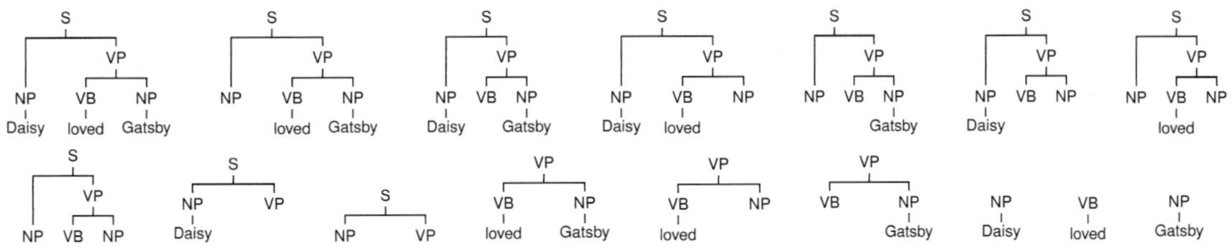

Figure 2: DOP1 fragments as extracted from the tree of "Daisy loved Gatsby."

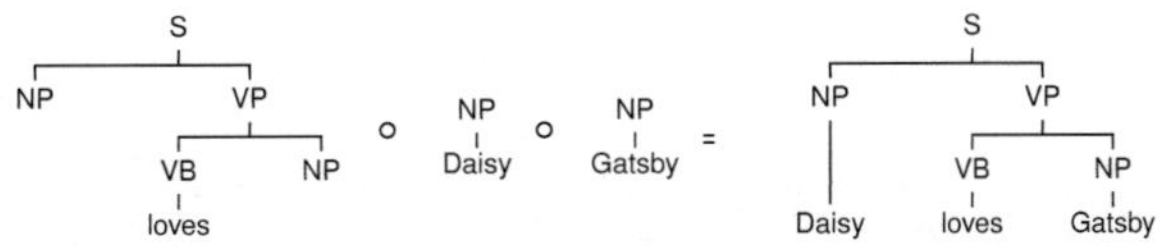

Figure 3: A DOP1 derivation. Note that "Daisy" becomes the subject, because fragments are combined with left-most substitution.

parser makes use of an agenda $\mathcal{A}$ (implemented as a priority queue with the decrease-key operation), a chart $\mathcal{C}$ with Viterbi probabilities, and the full chart $\mathcal{F}$ including suboptimal items. Both $\mathcal{A}$ and $\mathcal{C}$ store items I defined by a category and a span, paired with a weight x, while $\mathcal{F}$ stores weighted edges between items, representing a shared parse forest.

The algorithm is deceptively simple. Most of the work is in producing all items that can be deduced from a given item and items in the chart. This involves iterating over all grammar rules with matching labels, and verifying whether the yields of particular items can instantiate the rule. This can be optimized by representing yields as bit vectors and first verifying that the two yields do not overlap. The next step is to walk through both bit vectors in parallel and verifying the conditions for instantiating a rule. Rules that can be instantiated are given a score that is the sum of the weights (e.g., log probabilities) of their RHS.

Any LCFRS can be binarized (as required by the CKY parser) and parsed in $\mathcal{O}(|G| \cdot |w|^{3\varphi})$ time, where $|G|$ is the size of the grammar, $|w|$ is the length of the sentence, and φ is the fan-out after binarization (Gómez-Rodríguez et al., 2009). The fan-out may increase due to binarization, but in our experiments this was no cause for concern. The degree of the polynomial reflects the maximal number of comparisons needed to determine whether a rule can be applied; a binarized rule has three non-terminals with φ components each in the worst case.

This stands in contrast to previous formalisms for discontinuous parsing (Johnson, 1985; Plaehn, 2004), which have exponential time complexity. The difference is that in a LCFRS, the productions are formally context-free in the sense that they are applied without knowledge of the rest of the derivation, and they are restricted to cover certain spans in a particular order, which avoids having to enumerate the exponential number of possible discontinuous spans or permutations of the sentence.

4 Data-Oriented Parsing

Data-Oriented parsing (DOP) was introduced by Scha (1990) as both a cognitive and computational approach to analyzing language in terms of exemplars instead of rules. Concretely this works by allowing arbitrarily large fragments in the corpus to recombine with each other. The intuition is that, in terms of cognitive load, reuse is cheaper than computation, so remembering fragments is more effective than deriving them anew.

The first concrete DOP model was DOP1 (Bod, 1992). In DOP1, a fragment is defined as a connected subset of nodes in a tree, such that for every non-terminal node, the fragment either has all children in common with the tree, or none. In the latter case the node is a frontier node, which functions as a substitution site (this is analogous to an open slot in a construction). The weight of a fragment is its relative frequency in the training data. Figure 2 illustrates the DOP1 fragments extracted from the tree of an example sentence. Note that the smallest fragments

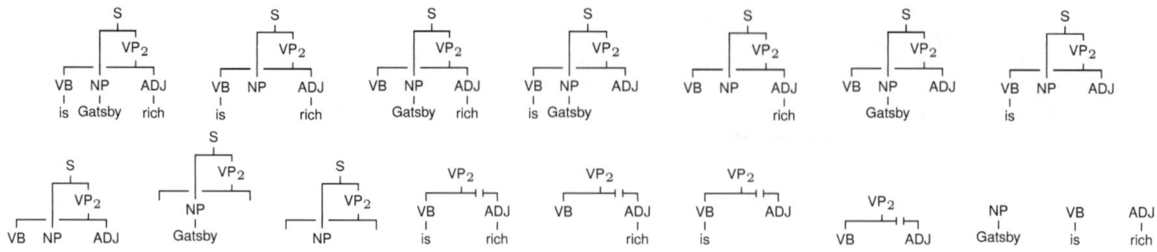

Figure 4: Discontinuous fragments as extracted from the tree of "is Gatsby rich?"

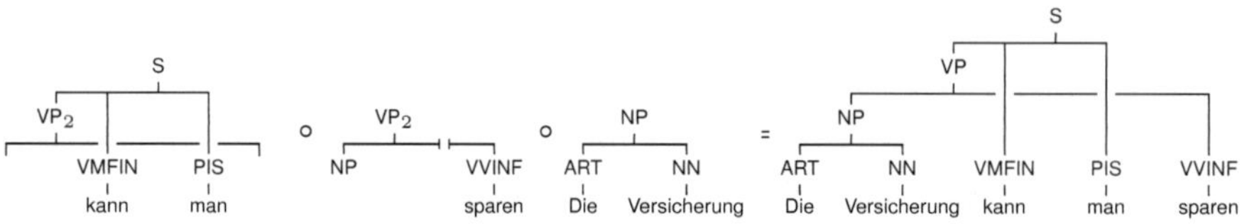

Figure 5: A discontinuous DOP derivation of the tree in figure 1.

correspond to CFG productions, such that a CFG is a DOP1 model restricted to fragments of depth 1.

A derivation is defined as a sequence of fragments combined through left-most substitution. Left-most substitution is defined for any two trees t_1 and t_2, such that t_1 has a frontier node labeled X and $\mathrm{root}(t_2) = X$; the result of $t_1 \circ t_2$ is a new tree where t_2 is substituted for the first frontier node labeled X in t_1. The probability of a derivation is the product of the weights of its fragments. Figure 3 shows a derivation with the fragments in figure 2.

We can generalize the DOP1 model to the case of discontinuous trees. By substituting an LCFRS for the CFG backbone of DOP1, we obtain a discontinuous DOP model—Disco-DOP. The Disco-DOP model employs the same definition of a fragment, but applies it to a broader class of trees. Figure 4 shows the fragments extracted from a discontinuous tree. Note that when a discontinuous node becomes a frontier node, it specifies where its yield will end up with respect to the yield of other nodes in the fragment. Figure 5 shows a derivation with discontinuous fragments of the tree in figure 1.

Parsing with all fragments explicitly is not possible, as there are exponentially many. One solution is to select a subset of fragments (e.g., Sangati and Zuidema, 2011). In this work we employ the approach introduced by Goodman (1996, 2003), who defines a PCFG which decomposes the probabilities of fragments into several PCFG productions, such that the same parse trees can be recovered as in a DOP model with explicitly represented fragments. This reduction generalizes straightforwardly to a PLCFRS.

Each node A in the training corpus is decorated with a unique address A_j. Given a node A_j with children B_k and C_l, the number of fragments headed by A_j is given by $a_j = (b_k + 1)(c_l + 1)$. The total number of subtrees (fragments) for A is given by $a = \sum_j a_j$. We also apply a normalization factor $\bar{a}$ which is the frequency of non-terminals of type A in the training data. The probabilities of Disco-DOP derivations can then be encoded in the following reduction, applied to each production in the training corpus:

$$\begin{array}{lcll}
A_j(\vec{\alpha}) & \rightarrow & B(\vec{\alpha_B})\ C(\vec{\alpha_C}) & (1/a_j) \\
A_j(\vec{\alpha}) & \rightarrow & B_k(\vec{\alpha_B})\ C(\vec{\alpha_C}) & (b_k/a_j) \\
A_j(\vec{\alpha}) & \rightarrow & B(\vec{\alpha_B})\ C_l(\vec{\alpha_C}) & (c_l/a_j) \\
A_j(\vec{\alpha}) & \rightarrow & B_k(\vec{\alpha_B})\ C_l(\vec{\alpha_C}) & (b_k c_l/a_j) \\
A(\vec{\alpha}) & \rightarrow & B(\vec{\alpha_B})\ C(\vec{\alpha_C}) & (1/(a\bar{a})) \\
A(\vec{\alpha}) & \rightarrow & B_k(\vec{\alpha_B})\ C(\vec{\alpha_C}) & (b_k/(a\bar{a})) \\
A(\vec{\alpha}) & \rightarrow & B(\vec{\alpha_B})\ C_l(\vec{\alpha_C}) & (c_l/(a\bar{a})) \\
A(\vec{\alpha}) & \rightarrow & B_k(\vec{\alpha_B})\ C_l(\vec{\alpha_C}) & (b_k c_l/(a\bar{a}))
\end{array}$$

Where $\vec{\alpha}$ refers to the arguments of the LHS non-terminal. Each addressed non-terminal represents an internal node of a fragment, while the unaddressed nodes represent both the root and the frontier nodes of fragments. The latter allow a switch from one fragment to another during parsing, viz. they simulate substitution sites of DOP fragments.

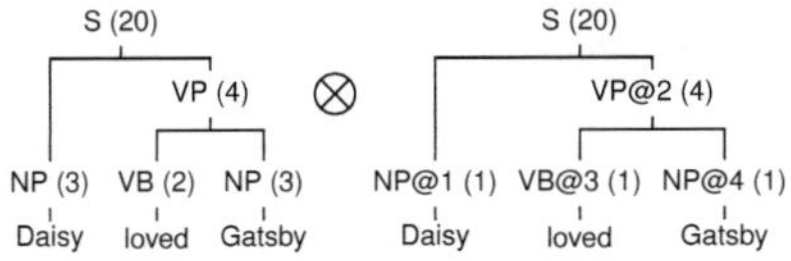

$^1/_{20}$	$S(x_0 x_1) \to NP(x_0)\ VP(x_1)$
$^4/_{20}$	$S(x_0 x_1) \to NP(x_0)\ VP@2(x_1)$
$^1/_{20}$	$S(x_0 x_1) \to NP@1(x_0)\ VP(x_1)$
$^4/_{20}$	$S(x_0 x_1) \to NP@1(x_0)\ VP@2(x_1)$
$^1/_4$	$VP(x_0 x_1) \to VB(x_0)\ NP(x_1)$
$^1/_4$	$VP(x_0 x_1) \to VB(x_0)\ NP@4(x_1)$
$^1/_4$	$VP(x_0 x_1) \to VB@3(x_0)\ NP(x_1)$
$^1/_4$	$VP(x_0 x_1) \to VB@3(x_0)\ NP@4(x_1)$
$^1/_4$	$VP@2(x_0 x_1) \to VB(x_0)\ NP(x_1)$
$^1/_4$	$VP@2(x_0 x_1) \to VB(x_0)\ NP@4(x_1)$
$^1/_4$	$VP@2(x_0 x_1) \to VB@3(x_0)\ NP(x_1)$
$^1/_4$	$VP@2(x_0 x_1) \to VB@3(x_0)\ NP@4(x_1)$
$^1/_3$	$NP(Daisy) \to \epsilon$
$^1/_1$	$NP@1(Daisy) \to \epsilon$
$^1/_2$	$VB(loved) \to \epsilon$
$^1/_1$	$VB@3(loved) \to \epsilon$
$^2/_3$	$NP(Gatsby) \to \epsilon$
$^1/_1$	$NP@4(Gatsby) \to \epsilon$

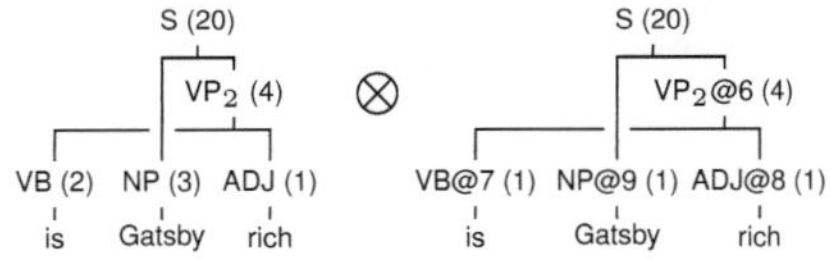

$^1/_{20}$	$S(x_0 x_2 x_1) \to VP_2(x_0, x_2)\ NP(x_2)$
$^1/_{20}$	$S(x_0 x_2 x_1) \to VP_2(x_0, x_2)\ NP@9(x_2)$
$^4/_{20}$	$S(x_0 x_2 x_1) \to VP_2@6(x_0, x_2)\ NP(x_2)$
$^4/_{20}$	$S(x_0 x_2 x_1) \to VP_2@6(x_0, x_2)\ NP@9(x_2)$
$^1/_4$	$VP_2(x_0, x_1) \to VB(x_0)\ ADJ(x_1)$
$^1/_4$	$VP_2(x_0, x_1) \to VB(x_0)\ ADJ@8(x_1)$
$^1/_4$	$VP_2(x_0, x_1) \to VB@7(x_0)\ ADJ(x_1)$
$^1/_4$	$VP_2(x_0, x_1) \to VB@7(x_0)\ ADJ@8(x_1)$
$^1/_4$	$VP_2@6(x_0, x_1) \to VB(x_0)\ ADJ(x_1)$
$^1/_4$	$VP_2@6(x_0, x_1) \to VB(x_0)\ ADJ@8(x_1)$
$^1/_4$	$VP_2@6(x_0, x_1) \to VB@7(x_0)\ ADJ(x_1)$
$^1/_4$	$VP_2@6(x_0, x_1) \to VB@7(x_0)\ ADJ@8(x_1)$
$^1/_1$	$ADJ(rich) \to \epsilon$
$^1/_1$	$ADJ@8(rich) \to \epsilon$
$^1/_1$	$NP@9(Gatsby) \to \epsilon$
$^1/_2$	$VB(is) \to \epsilon$
$^1/_1$	$VB@7(is) \to \epsilon$

Figure 6: The pairwise Cartesian product of the productions in the original and the addressed tree gives the productions in the reduction.

The use of the normalization factor is called the Equal Weights Estimate; this formulation follows Bod (2003). Goodman (2003) first suggested this normalization but his formula appears to contain a mistake, having a_j in the denominator of the last four rules instead of a. The normalization is intended to counter the bias for large subtrees in DOP1—when all fragments are considered, the majority will consist of large fragments, which results in the majority of probability mass being assigned to rare, large fragments.

Intuitively, the reduction can be seen as state-splitting in the limit. A state-split partitions a non-terminal into two or more new non-terminals to cover more specific and fine-grained contexts. Taken to the extreme, we can keep splitting non-terminals until each resulting non-terminal refers to one specific occurrence of that non-terminal in a single sentence, which greatly increases the amount of hierarchical information that can be extracted and exploited from the training corpus. This is exactly what happens in Goodman's reduction. Compared to other automatic state-splitting approaches such as latent variable grammars, this approach has the advantage of being conceptually much simpler.

Figure 6 shows a concrete example of the reduction, using the tree from figure 1. The eight productions per node of the reduction can be considered as the pairwise Cartesian product of the original production and the one with addressed nodes. To get the reduction of a complete tree, this operation is applied to all productions of both trees in parallel. The probabilities are derived from the number of subtrees, shown in brackets after the node labels. The normalization step has been left out, for simplicity's sake. Productions without addressed nodes, i.e., the original productions, will recur, and their probabilities must be summed. In our case productions are considered equivalent when both the non-terminals and their arguments match.

The large number of non-terminals and productions in this grammar make parsing with this reduction inefficient. In order to optimize parsing with the DOP reduction, we apply coarse-to-fine inference in the spirit of Bansal and Klein (2010). The principle is to parse first with a coarse grammar, in this case the treebank PLCFRS, and use information from the resulting chart to prune parsing with the full grammar, in this case the DOP reduction. Figure 7 illustrates the approach. The fine grammar is *projected* onto the coarse grammar by mapping nodes A_j to the original nodes A. Pruning is implemented by blocking items $\langle A, \vec{a} \rangle$ which are not part of the n-best derivations in the coarse chart; such items are simply prevented from entering the agenda. Although this approach is reminiscent of re-ranking (Charniak and Johnson, 2005), in our approach items can recombine to form parse trees not present in the n-best derivations. We use $n = 50$ in all experiments.

We aim at maximizing the chance of obtaining the correct structure for a given sentence, viz. finding its

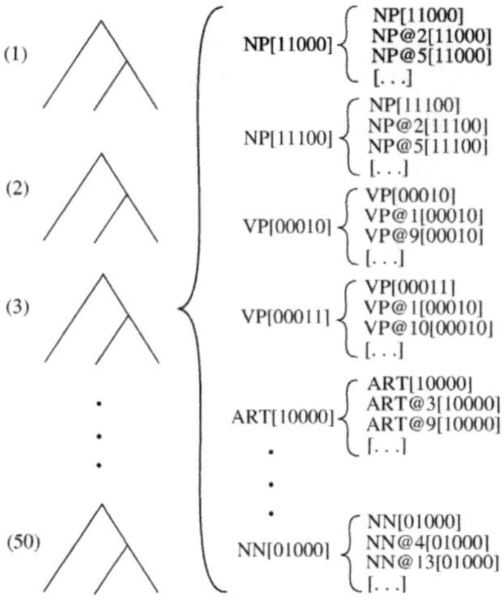

Figure 7: The coarse-to-fine inference. On the left are the n-best derivations from the coarse chart. In the middle the chart items (category and spans) extracted from those derivations. On the right are all items for the fine grammar that map to these coarse items. The latter will be the only items allowed to enter the agenda when parsing with the fine grammar.

most probable parse (MPP). In DOP the probability of a parse tree is the sum of all its possible derivations. However, as there can be exponentially many derivations for each parse tree, finding the MPP is NP-hard (Sima'an, 1996). Therefore the MPP must be approximated with a restricted set of derivations: a list of derivations is produced using the algorithm of Huang and Chiang (2005) which efficiently extracts the exact k-best list from an exhaustive chart with Viterbi probabilities. We use $k = 10,000$ in all experiments. After this list is obtained, we sum the probabilities of all derivations generating the same parse tree by applying the projection, and select the best one. Note that probabilities of DOP derivations are spread over multiple derivations in Goodman's reduction. In our experiments the list of derivations in the reduction often collapses to just 5 parse trees.

words	train	test	PLCFRS rules	Disco-DOP rules
≤ 15	9025	1015	24020	678659
≤ 25	14870	1639	53773	1769507
≤ 30	16490	1845	50381	1799797

Table 1: Number of sentences and rules.

5 Experiments

We evaluate on version 2 of the German Negra treebank (Skut et al., 1997). Results are for models based on splits of 90% training data and 10% test data. The setup follows Kallmeyer and Maier (2010) as much as possible. The parser is presented with (gold) part-of-speech tags from the treebank. The DOP model, however, does exploit its knowledge of lexical dependencies by using fragments with terminals. In a pre-processing step, function labels are discarded and all punctuation is lowered to the best matching constituent. Heads are marked using the head finding rules for the Negra corpus used by the Stanford parser, after which trees are binarized head-outward (Klein and Manning, 2003a,b). The markovization setting is v=1 (i.e., no parent annotation), and $h \in \{1, 2, \infty\}$, dictated by efficiency concerns. Lower values for h give better performance because they allow more flat structures to be covered through re-combinations of parts of different constituents. However, this also greatly increases the number of possible edges which have to be explored. For this reason we had to increase the value of h for parsing longer sentences, at the cost of decreased performance and coverage. Figure 8 illustrates the binarization. With these settings the grammar has a fan-out of 5 for the grammar of up to 15 word sentences, and a fan-out of 7 for the other two. Table 1 lists the size of the training & test corpora and their grammars for the respective length restrictions. Note that Kallmeyer and Maier (2010) apply the length restriction before the 90-10 split, but the difference is not more than 12 sentences.

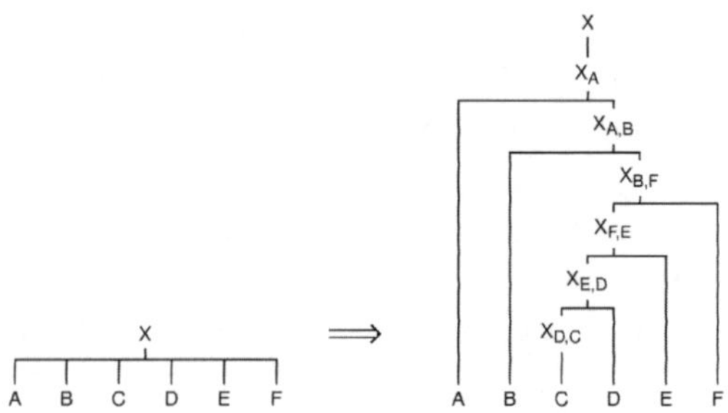

Figure 8: A head-outward binarization with h=2 v=1 markovization; C is the head node.

NEGRA	words	coverage	LP	LR	F1	EX
Plaehn (2004): DPSG	≤ 15	96.04	73.61	72.72	73.16	39.0
Kallmeyer and Maier (2010): PLCFRS	≤ 15	-	-	-	81.27	-
This work: Disco-DOP v=1, h=1	≤ 15	99.90	84.09	85.03	**84.56**	54.68
Kallmeyer and Maier (2010): PLCFRS	≤ 25	99.45	73.03	73.46	73.25	-
This work: Disco-DOP v=1, h=2	≤ 25	98.90	78.26	79.37	**78.81**	39.11
Maier and Kallmeyer (2010): PLCFRS	≤ 30	97.00	72.39	70.68	71.52	-
This work: Disco-DOP v=1, h=∞	≤ 30	96.59	73.05	74.93	**73.98**	34.80

Table 2: Results for discontinuous parsing on the Negra treebank.

Evaluation is performed using a generalization of the PARSEVAL measures, which compares bracketings of the form $\langle A, \vec{a}\rangle$ where $\vec{a}$ is the yield described by a tuple of intervals (Maier, 2010); we used Maier's publicly available implementation.[2] We use PARSEVAL, in spite of its serious shortcomings (Rehbein and van Genabith, 2007), to enable comparison with previous work. Unparsed sentences are assigned a baseline parse with all tags directly under the root node.

Our model performs consistently better than previous results on discontinuous parsing; see table 2 for the results, including comparisons to previous work. Figure 9 plots the time required to parse sentences of different lengths with v=1 h=2, showing a strikingly steep curve, which makes clear why parsing sentences longer than 25 words was not feasible with these settings. The coarse-to-fine inference appears to work rather well, apparently displaying a linear observed time complexity on the DOP grammar; unfortunately exhaustive parsing with the coarse grammar forms a bottleneck. The total time to parse was 1, 16 and 52 hours for 15, 25, and 30 words respectively, using about 4 GB of memory.

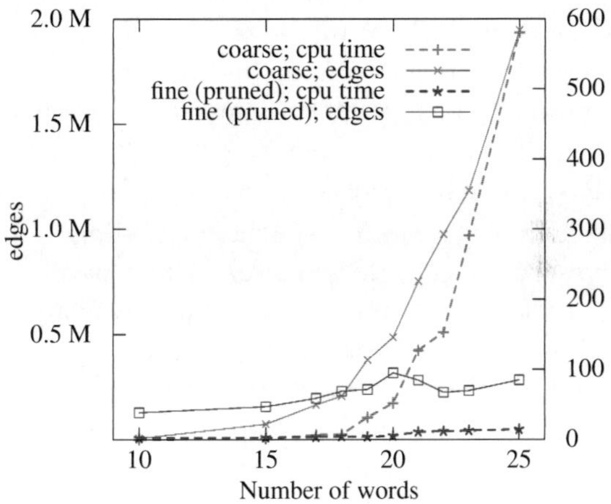

Figure 9: Efficiency as a function of the number of words in the coarse (PLCFRS) and the fine stage (Disco-DOP).The data are from parsing 10 Negra sentences, hand-picked to illustrate the worst case.

6 Remaining challenges

From these results it may appear as if the combination of the formalism and treebank parsing forms an inherent barrier to parsing longer sentences. Even Kallmeyer and Maier (2010), who employ a precomputed table of outside estimates, could not parse beyond 30 words, because of memory limitations. Their four-dimensional table is indexed on non-terminals, span length, length of gaps, and number of words to the left and right. This implies a space complexity of $\mathcal{O}(|N|\cdot n^3)$ where $|N|$ is the number of non-terminals and n the maximum sentence length. With approximately 12,000 non-terminals as cited by Kallmeyer and Maier (2010), a limit of 100 words per sentence, and double precision, this implies a table of 96 GB.

Another issue is that it is not clear whether obtaining k-best lists with these estimates works well or is possible at all. Pauls and Klein (2009) present an algorithm for extending an A* parser to a parser that builds the k-best derivations during parsing, but the estimates of Kallmeyer and Maier (2010) are not monotone, a property which is assumed by Pauls and Klein (2009). Monotonicity guarantees that the Viterbi parse will be found first.

We consider extending the coarse-to-fine approach to be more promising. Instead of only making the

[2] Cf. http://www.wolfgang-maier.net/rparse

categories coarser, we can also resort to a coarser formalism. Following Barthélemy et al. (2001), we can extract a grammar that defines a superset of the language we want to parse, but with a fan-out of 1. Concretely, a context-free grammar can be read off from discontinuous trees that have been transformed to context-free trees by the procedure introduced by Boyd (2007). Each discontinuous node is split into a set of new nodes, one for each component; for example a node NP_2 will be split into two nodes labeled NP*1 and NP*2 (like Barthélemy et al., we can mark components with an index to reduce overgeneration). Because Boyd's transformation is reversible, derivations from this grammar can be converted back to discontinuous trees, and can guide parsing with the LCFRS. Results with this approach will be reported in future work.

Aside from these technical issues, many linguistic features have been glossed over in this work to limit its scope. A proper parser and evaluation should work with grammatical functions as well, and parsing languages with less strict word-order implies that morphology provides important information about constituents that have been moved or extraposed. Movement and extraposition could also be modeled statistically, which can reduce data sparsity. Scrambling is known to be beyond the power of LCFRS (Becker et al., 1992); however, the question is whether it needs to be part of the formalism at all. As the work of Tsarfaty (2010) shows, it is possible to incorporate morphology, grammatical functions, and word-order in a statistical model built on a PCFG backbone. Perhaps this approach could be combined with the work presented here, such that it can produce discontinuous structures using LCFRS, and to weaken its independence assumptions through a DOP model.

7 Conclusion

A data-oriented model of discontinuous phrase-structure has been presented which outperforms all previously published results. This has been achieved by combining a variety of techniques: a linear context-free rewriting system as the symbolic grammar, data-oriented parsing as the probabilistic framework, a general method for enumerating k-best derivations from a chart, and a coarse-to-fine optimization to tame the complexity of DOP.

It turns out that using a grammar formalism with a parsing complexity that is well beyond cubic is not an impediment for making a DOP model with considerably better performance. The remaining difficulty with parsing longer sentences lies squarely on the side of discontinuity, not DOP. It is quite plausible that further innovations in binarization, pruning and estimates will enable parsing longer sentences.

Acknowledgments

We are grateful to Wolfgang Maier for correspondence and making the code of his parser `rparse` available.

References

Mohit Bansal and Dan Klein. 2010. Simple, accurate parsing with an all-fragments grammar. In *Proceedings of ACL*, pages 1098–1107.

François Barthélemy, Pierre Boullier, Philippe Deschamp, and Éric de la Clergerie. 2001. Guided parsing of range concatenation languages. In *Proceedings of ACL*, pages 42–49.

Tilman Becker, Owen Rambow, and Michael Niv. 1992. The derivational generative power of formal systems or scrambling is beyond LCFRS. Technical Report IRCS-92-38, Institute for research in cognitive science. URL `ftp://ftp.cis.upenn.edu/pub/ircs/tr/92-38.ps.Z`.

Stefan Behnel, Robert Bradshaw, Craig Citro, Lisandro Dalcin, Dag Sverre Seljebotn, and Kurt Smith. 2011. Cython: The best of both worlds. *Computing in Science and Engineering*, 13:31–39.

Steven Bird, Ewan Klein, and Edward Loper. 2009. *Natural Language Processing with Python*. O'Reilly Media.

Rens Bod. 1992. A computational model of language performance: Data-oriented parsing. In *Proceedings COLING'92 (Nantes, France)*, pages 855–859.

Rens Bod. 2003. An efficient implementation of a new DOP model. In *Proceedings of EACL*, volume 1, pages 19–26. URL `http://www.ldc.upenn.edu/acl/E/E03/E03-1005.pdf`.

Pierre Boullier. 1998. Proposal for a natural language processing syntactic backbone. Technical Report RR-3342, INRIA-Rocquencourt, Le Chesnay, France. URL http://www.inria.fr/RRRT/RR-3342.html.

Adriane Boyd. 2007. Discontinuity revisited: An improved conversion to context-free representations. In *Proceedings of the Linguistic Annotation Workshop*, pages 41–44.

Sabine Brants, Stefanie Dipper, Silvia Hansen, Wolfgang Lezius, and George Smith. 2002. The Tiger treebank. In *Proceedings of the workshop on treebanks and linguistic theories*, pages 24–41.

Eugene Charniak and Mark Johnson. 2005. Coarse-to-fine n-best parsing and maxent discriminative reranking. In *Proceedings of ACL*, pages 173–180.

Noam Chomsky. 1957. *Syntactic Structures*. Mouton, The Hague.

Carlos Gómez-Rodríguez, Marco Kuhlmann, Giorgio Satta, and David Weir. 2009. Optimal reduction of rule length in linear context-free rewriting systems. In *Proceedings of NAACL HLT 2009*, pages 539–547.

Joshua Goodman. 1996. Efficient algorithms for parsing the DOP model. In *Proceedings of EMNLP*, pages 143–152.

Joshua Goodman. 2003. Efficient parsing of DOP with PCFG-reductions. In Rens Bod, Remko Scha, and Khalil Sima'an, editors, *Data-Oriented Parsing*. The University of Chicago Press.

Liang Huang and David Chiang. 2005. Better k-best parsing. In *Proceedings of IWPT 2009*, pages 53–64.

Mark Johnson. 1985. Parsing with discontinuous constituents. In *Proceedings of ACL*, pages 127–132.

Laura Kallmeyer and Wolfgang Maier. 2010. Data-driven parsing with probabilistic linear context-free rewriting systems. In *Proceedings of the 23rd International Conference on Computational Linguistics*, pages 537–545.

Dan Klein and Christopher D. Manning. 2003a. Accurate unlexicalized parsing. In *Proceedings of ACL*, volume 1, pages 423–430.

Dan Klein and Christopher D. Manning. 2003b. Fast exact inference with a factored model for natural language parsing. *Advances in neural information processing systems*, pages 3–10.

Wolfgang Maier. 2010. Direct parsing of discontinuous constituents in German. In *Proceedings of the SPMRL workshop at NAACL HLT 2010*, pages 58–66.

Wolfgang Maier and Laura Kallmeyer. 2010. Discontinuity and non-projectivity: Using mildly contextsensitive formalisms for data-driven parsing. In *Proceedings of TAG*, volume 10.

Wolfgang Maier and Anders Søgaard. 2008. Treebanks and mild context-sensitivity. In *Proceedings of Formal Grammar 2008*, page 61.

Mark-Jan Nederhof. 2003. Weighted deductive parsing and Knuth's algorithm. *Computational Linguistics*, 29(1):135–143.

Adam Pauls and Dan Klein. 2009. K-best A* parsing. In *Proceedings of ACL*, volume 2, pages 958–966.

Oliver Plaehn. 2004. Computing the most probable parse for a discontinuous phrase structure grammar. In Harry Bunt, John Carroll, and Giorgio Satta, editors, *New developments in parsing technology*, pages 91–106. Kluwer Academic Publishers, Norwell, MA, USA.

Ines Rehbein and Josef van Genabith. 2007. Evaluating evaluation measures. In *NODALIDA 2007 Conference Proceedings*, pages 372–379. URL http://doras.dcu.ie/15237.

Federico Sangati and Willem Zuidema. 2011. Accurate parsing with compact tree-substitution grammars: Double-DOP. In *Proceedings of EMNLP*, pages 84–95. URL http://www.aclweb.org/anthology/D11-1008.

Walter J. Savitch, Emmon Bach, W. Marsh, and Gila Safran-Naveh. 1987. *The Formal Complexity of Natural Language*, volume 33 of *Linguistics and Philosophy*. D. Reidel.

Remko Scha. 1990. Language theory and language technology; competence and performance. In Q.A.M. de Kort and G.L.J. Leerdam, editors, *Computertoepassingen in de Neerlandistiek*, pages 7–22. LVVN, Almere, the Netherlands.

Original title: *Taaltheorie en taaltechnologie; competence en performance*. Translation available at http://iaaa.nl/rs/LeerdamE.html.

Stuart M. Shieber. 1985. Evidence against the context-freeness of natural language. *Linguistics and Philosophy*, 8:333–343.

Khalil Sima'an. 1996. Computational complexity of probabilistic disambiguation by means of tree-grammars. In *Proceedings of the 16th conference on Computational linguistics*, volume 2, pages 1175–1180.

Wojciech Skut, Brigitte Krenn, Thorten Brants, and Hans Uszkoreit. 1997. An annotation scheme for free word order languages. In *Proceedings of ANLP*, pages 88–95.

Ann Taylor, Mitchell Marcus, and Beatrice Santorini. 2003. The penn treebank: an overview. In Anne Abeillé, editor, *Treebanks: Building and using parsed corpora*, pages 5–22. Springer.

Reut Tsarfaty. 2010. *Relational-realizational parsing*. Ph.D. thesis, University of Amsterdam. URL http://dare.uva.nl/record/335795.

K. Vijay-Shanker, David J. Weir, and Aravind K. Joshi. 1987. Characterizing structural descriptions produced by various grammatical formalisms. In *Proceedings of ACL*, pages 104–111.

Multiword Expressions in Statistical Dependency Parsing

Gülşen Eryiğit **Tugay İlbay** **Ozan Arkan Can**
Department of Computer Engineering
Istanbul Technical University
Istanbul, 34469, Turkey
{gulsen.cebiroglu,ilbay, cano}@itu.edu.tr

Abstract

In this paper, we investigated the impact of extracting different types of multiword expressions (MWEs) in improving the accuracy of a data-driven dependency parser for a morphologically rich language (Turkish). We showed that in the training stage, the unification of MWEs of a certain type, namely compound verb and noun formations, has a negative effect on parsing accuracy by increasing the lexical sparsity. Our results gave a statistically significant improvement by using a variant of the treebank excluding this MWE type in the training stage. Our extrinsic evaluation of an ideal MWE recognizer (for only extracting MWEs of type named entities, duplications, numbers, dates and some predefined list of compound prepositions) showed that the preprocessing of the test data would improve the labeled parsing accuracy by 1.5%.

1 Introduction

Multiword expressions are compound word formations formed by two or more words. They generally represent a different meaning than the words which compose them. The importance of detecting multiword expressions in different NLP problems is emphasized by many researchers and is still a topic which is being investigated for different NLP layers (Kordoni et al., 2011). It is impossible to neglect the importance for machine translation where the translation of a MWE would be totally different than the translation of its constituents. But the effect of different MWE types on parsing accuracy is still an open research topic and needs to be analyzed in detail.

Hogan et al. (2011) recently give their preliminary results on detecting named-entities and reports no improvement in parsing accuracy for English. Nivre and Nilsson (2004) reports a 5% parsing accuracy increase for Swedish by using a depedency parser which uses a memory-based learner as its oracle. In this study, they only focus on multiword names and compound function words. Cafferkey (2008) reports very small (falling short of their initial expectations) but statistically significant improvements for a PCFG parser (on English). Korkontzelos and Manandhar (2010) reports an improvement of sentence accuracy 7.5% in shallow parsing by concentrating on MWE of types compound nominals, proper names and adjective noun constructions. The conflicting results and the difference in success ranges may be caused by many factors; such as the parsing paradigm, the language in focus, the MWE types used in the experiments and the evaluation metrics.

In this study, we are making a detailed investigation of extracting different MWE classes as a preprocessing step for a statistical dependency parser (MaltParser v1.5.1 Nivre et al. (2007)). We conducted our experiments on Turkish Dependency Treebanks (Oflazer et al., 2003, Eryiğit, 2007). We semi-automatically created different versions of the data by manually annotating and classifying MWEs. We made an in depth analysis of using the new treebank versions both on training and testing stages. We evaluated the parser's performance both on MWEs and the remaining parts of the sentences.

Our results showed that different MWE types have different impacts on the parsing accuracy. For Turkish, we showed that the preprocessing of compound verb and noun formations causes a considerable decrease in accuracy. We also demonstrated that a MWE extractor which finds the MWEs from the remaining types would make a significant improvement for parsing. For now, it is not possible to generalize the results for other languages and parsing paradigms. But we believe, we present a systematic approach for evaluating the scenario.

2 Motivation

Eryigit et al. (2008) in their article "Dependency Parsing of Turkish" points out to a decrease of nearly 4 percentage points when they test their parser on the raw data. Although they only look at this decrease from the point of the errors caused by parts-of-speech (POS) tagging, the decrease could actually be due to two reasons: 1. The errors caused by the automatic POS tagging, 2. The lack of MWE handling which exists in the gold standard. In this study, we will focus on to the second item and on the improvement that could be reached by handling MWEs. With this purpose, we are asking and answering the following questions during the remaining of the paper:

1. What is the success of available MWE extractors on detecting the MWEs manually annotated in the treebank?
2. When we analyze the "false positives"[1] of the MWE extractors, we see that most of them are actually valid MWEs. Should we as well manually annotate these in the treebanks?
3. When we decide to annotate these MWEs[2], the results of the automatic parsing become worse then the previous results with the original treebank. Should we concentrate on different MWE types?

The paper is structured as follows: Section 3 makes a short description of the Turkish language. Section 4 presents the configuration used in our experiments. Section 5 gives our experimental results. Section 6 gives our conclusion and comments for future works.

3 Turkish

Turkish is an agglutinative language with a very rich morphological structure. The dependencies between the words constructing a sentence is almost entirely head-final in the written text. The derivational and inflectional richness of the language results in shorter sentence lengths when compared to other languages (8.16 words/sentence[3]). In similar studies, the Turkish words are most of the time analyzed as a sequence of one or more inflectional groups (IGs). Each IG consists of either a stem or a derivational suffix plus all the inflectional suffixes belonging to that stem/derivational suffix. The head of a whole word is not just another word but a specific IG of another word. Figure 1 shows the IGs in a simple sentence: "küçük odadayım" (*I'm in the small room*). The word "odadayım" is formed from two IGs; a verb is derived from an inflected noun "odada" (*in the room*). In the example, the adjective "küçük" (*small*) should be connected to the first IG of the second word. It is the word "oda" (*room*) which is modified by the adjective, not the derived verb form "odadayım" (*I'm in the room*). So both the correct head word and the correct IG in the head word should be determined by the parser.

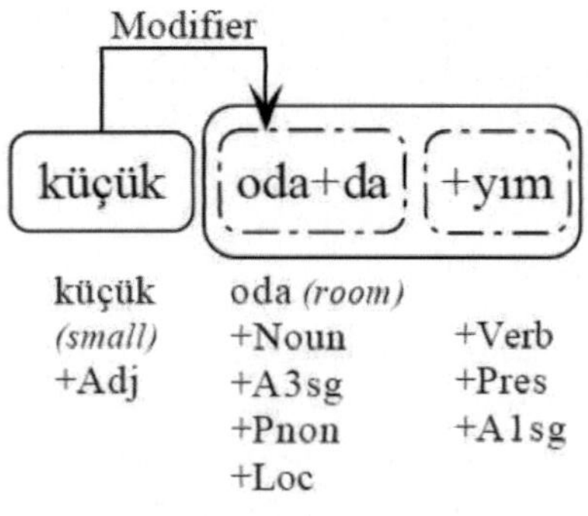

Figure 1: Word and dependency representations
A1sg = 1sg number/person agreement, A3sg = 3sg number/person agreement, Loc = Locative case, Pnon = No possessive agreement, Pres = Present Tense

These properties of the language makes it very

[1] the group of words which are tagged as MWEs by the automatic analyzers but not in the current treebanks (somehow missed by the human annotators).

[2] described in the 2nd item

[3] where the number differs between 13.16-27.7 for other languages (Nivre et al., 2007)

hard for dependency parsing[4]. Buchholz and Marsi (2006) reports the Turkish Treebank having the highest number of different surface forms and the second with new lemma within 13 different languages. As a result, any change on lexical representation could end up with severe lexical sparsity problems.

4 Configuration

4.1 Parser

We are using MaltParser v1.5.1 (Nivre et al., 2007) which is a data-driven dependency parser whose success is reported to be very high across a variety of different languages (Nivre et al., 2006). For the repeatability of the results we used exactly the same feature representation and parser options from Eryigit et al. (2008) . The cited reference gives these options in details so we do not repeat them here again. The parser's current version uses a support vector machine (SVM) classifier for predicting the parser's actions. The usage of SVM in this area has been proven to be very successful. And we know that the parser's capability is very high at learning many syntactic structures especially the ones with shorter distances. In the following sections, we will see that the extraction of MWE types where the parser is already good at determining have a negative effect on parsing accuracy by increasing the lexical sparsity.

4.2 Data Sets

In our experiments, we are using the METU-Sabancı Turkish Treebank (Oflazer et al., 2003) which consists of 5635 sentences (in Conll format). The second column of Table 1 gives the statistics for the original treebank (Vo); there exist 2040 MWEs which are manually combined into single units. Figure 2-a gives the symbolic representation of MWEs in the original treebank. In the figure, w1 w2 w3 are the three constituents of a MWE and are collapsed into a single unit (by the use of underscores) which acts as a single word in the dependency structure. We created 3 new versions of the treebank:

1. Detached Version (Vd): is the version where the annotated MWEs are detached and a new

[4]Interested reader may refer to Eryigit et al. (2008) for detailed examples.

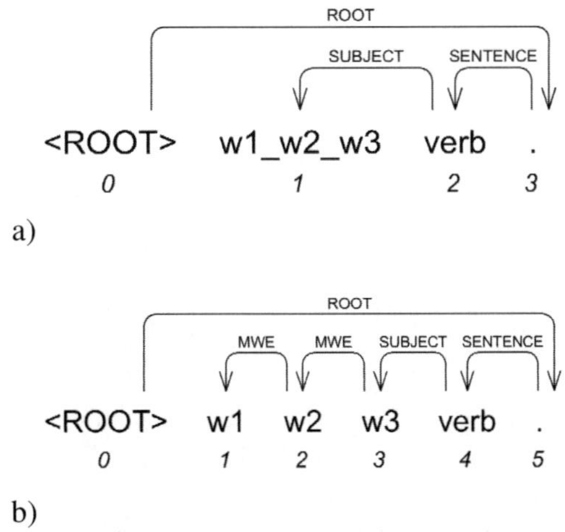

Figure 2: MWE representation in the Turkish Treebank *(picture drawn with MaltEval TreeViewer(Nilsson and Nivre, 2008))*

dependency type "MWE" is created between the MWE constituents (Figure 2-b). The strategy that is adopted while creating these dependencies is to connect the last IG of the dependent to the first IG of the head except for compound functional words (explained later in this section). In the treebank, the gold-standard POS tag and inflectional features given for the MWE in focus is only valid for the last constituent of that MWE. After the detachment process, we need to assign the correct tags (token index, lemma, surface form, postag, inflectional features, dependency type and head index) to the new coming IGs (words are constructed from one or more IGs each having their own tags). In order to select the correct postags, we passed these words from a morphological analyzer (Oflazer, 1994) and then manually disambiguated the ones having more than one possible analyses (1265/2437 words). After this stage, we created the new tags, inserted them to the sentences and renumbered the token indices, incoming and outgoing dependencies within the remaining of the sentence.

2. Enlarged Version (Ve): We needed to create the following two versions of the treebank during the evaluation of the automatic MWE extractors that will be introduced in the following section. In order to create version Ve,

Version	Turkish Treebank *Vo*	*Vd*	*Ve*	*Ve-o*	Validation Set
# of sentences	5635	5635	5635	5635	300
# of tokens	65184	67803	63318	65887	4513
# of words inc. punctuations	53992	56424	52267	54642	3610
# of words exc. punctuations	43572	45999	41847	44217	3080
# of combined collocations	2040	0	3674	1697	89

Table 1: Data sets' statistics: Version (Vo - Version Original; Vd - Version detached; Ve - Version enlarged; Ve-o - Version enlarged excluding the combined collocations of Vo)

we first extracted a MWE list consisting the 30150 MWEs available in the Turkish Dictionary (TDK, 2011) and then automatically listed the entire treebank sentences where the lemmas of the co-occurring words could match[5] the lemmas of the MWE constituents in the list. We manually marked the sentences where the co-occurring words may be actually accepted as a MWE (but somehow missed during the construction of the treebanks) and then automatically combined these words into single units and renumbered the token indices and incoming and outgoing dependencies within the remaining of the sentence. By this process, 1697 new MWEs are added to the treebank (Table 1).

3. Version Ve-o: is the treebank version where only the MWEs coming from the dictionary are annotated over the detached version. In other words, the annotated MWEs in Ve-o is the relative complement of Vo in Ve.[6]

Table1 gives the statistics for all the versions and the validation set (Eryiğit, 2007). We see from the table that different versions change the number of tokens and dependencies that should be discovered by the parser; as an example Vd increases the dependency number that will be evaluated from 43572 to 45999. In Table 1, the difference between # of combined collocations 1697 and 3674-2040 are due to overlapping MWEs consisting 2 or more words.

In the Turkish Treebank, there exists a very small amount (54) of compound functional words which are combined into a single unit. These are mostly the conjunctions which has an extra -da/-de/-ki enclitics written on the right side of and separately from the conjunction they attach to. We see that since these head-initial dependencies do not obey the general head-final dependency tradition of the treebank, only this type of compound functional words are preferred to be combined into single units in the construction phase of the treebank. While creating the detached version, we only process these differently and detach them in a head-initial manner.[7] Figure 3 shows the detachment for the "ya da" (*or*) conjunction.

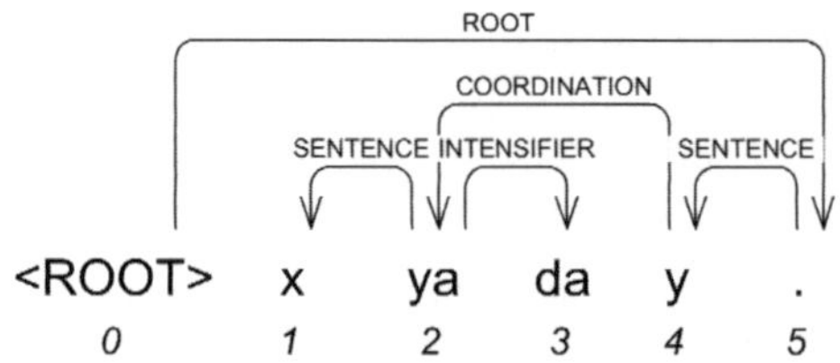

Figure 3: The detachment of Combined Functional Words

4.3 MWE Extractors

In order to understand the structure of the data in hand and the behavior of the current MWE extractors on it, we evaluated the success of two different MWE extractors. Table 2 gives the precision, recall and F values. All the experiments have been conducted on the detached version of the treebank and evaluated both on the original and enlarged versions.

[5]The lemmas of the words in the treebank are gold-standard. But in order to create the possible lemmas for the MWE constituents of the dictionary list, we used a morphological analyzer.

[6]Thus this version similarly to the version Vd, consists also a new dependency label "MWE".

[7]In our preliminary tests, we have detached these as regular MWEs and observed that the parser tends to find the actually correct dependencies but we penalize it unnecessarily.

The first MWE extractor is the rule based processor of Oflazer et al. (2004). For the second one, we developed a MWE checker by using the dictionary MWE list described in the previous section. Due to the inflectional structure of Turkish, MWE constituent words go under inflection as well. That's why we tried 3 different models while catching the MWEs in the treebank:

- Model 0: The co-occurring words in the treebank sentences are accepted as a MWE if and only if they have the exact surface forms with the MWE's constituents in the dictionary list.
- Model 1: Only the last constituent of the MWE is allowed to go under inflection (the ones at the beginning should have exactly the same surface form).
- Model 2: All of the constituents are allowed to be inflected.

		Ofl.(2004)	Mod.0	Mod.1	Mod.2
Vo	P	57.27	27.54	35.00	28.43
	R	30.93	12.22	46.29	49.48
	F	40.17	16.93	39.86	36.11
Ve	P	75.09	90.15	84.93	73.52
	R	22.54	22.24	62.45	71.15
	F	34.68	35.68	71.97	72.32

Table 2: Performance of MWE Extractors: Ofl.(2004):the MWE processor of Oflazer et al. (2004);Mod.x:Model x

We see from Table 2 that the results of the evaluation by using the version Vo is very low than expected; the highest F score that could be obtained with Ofl.(2004) is 40.17 and the dictionary list is 39.86. When we look at the cause, we notice that many of the compound verb and noun formations in the Turkish Dictionary are not marked in the original treebank and that causes very low precision scores (Mod.0 27.54). In order to alleviate this problem and with the hope to achieve better results in parsing accuracy, we created the version Ve of the treebank described in the previous section. By evaluating with this new version of the treebank, we see that the precision values are increased drastically for all of the models; Ofl.(2004) from 57.27 $\rightarrow$ 75.09, Mod.0 from 27.54 $\rightarrow$ 90.15. The recalls are still low for many of the models; Mod.2 with the highest recall value. The next section will search the answer of the question what will happen to the parsing performance if we develop a perfect MWE recognizer with an F score of 100%.

5 Experiments

We have four sets of experiments. Before introducing them, we will first explain our evaluation strategy.

5.1 Evaluation Metrics

We exactly follow the evaluation metrics used in Eryigit et al. (2008): We use ten-fold cross-validation in the experiments on the treebank (except the experiments on the validation set). We report the results as mean scores of the ten-fold cross-validation, with standard error. The main evaluation metrics that we use are the unlabeled attachment score (AS_U) and labeled attachment score (AS_L), namely, the proportion of IGs that are attached to the correct head (with the correct label for AS_L). A correct attachment is one in which the dependent IG (the last IG in the dependent word) is not only attached to the correct head word but also to the correct IG within the head word. We also report the (unlabeled) word-to-word score (WW_U), which only measures whether a dependent word is connected to (some IG in) the correct head word. We will refer to this metric (WW_U) especially while evaluating the dependencies between MWEs' constituents since we are automatically creating these dependencies (thus automatically selecting the IG to which the dependent will be connected). Where relevant, we also test the statistical significance of the results.

5.2 Evaluation Type

In order to see the impact of different approaches, we are making 3 different evaluations:

1. overall; AS_U, AS_L, WW_U scores provided
2. the dependencies with "MWE" labels (appearing after the detachment of MWE units Figure 2-b): AS_U, precision, recall, WW_U scores provided
3. the dependencies excluding the ones with "MWE" labels (the surrounding structure in the sentence): AS_U, AS_L, WW_U scores provided

5.3 Experiment Set I

In this set of experiments we first repeated the results of Eryigit at al. (2008) with the new Maltparser version. And then, tested the trained model on the different treebank versions that we had prepared. The first two lines of Table 3 gives the results reported in Eryigit at al. (2008); the second line is their results on the raw data where the pos tagging has been done by using an automatic analyzer. The fourth line gives our results when we test our parser on the detached version of the treebank. We see that our results on this version are better than the results obtained with raw data (73.3 - 74.7 AS_U) since we are using gold standard pos tags in order to be able to focus on the errors caused by the lack of MWE annotation. So, if we compare the tests on Vo with Vd, we see that the parser's performance drops from 76.1 to 74.7 (-1.4) in AS_U, 83.0 to 81.8 (-1.2) in WW_U and 67.4 to 63.3 (-4.1) in AS_L. We provide two values for the labeled accuracy on Vd: Since there is not any dependency with "MWE" label in the training model trained with the original treebank, it is impossible for the parser to assign correct labels to this kind of dependencies. If we accept all the labels assigned to these dependencies as correct than we will obtain a labeled accuracy of 66.5 given after the slash in the AS_L cell. And in this case, the drop in labeled accuracy would be 0.9. Of course this is a very optimistic evaluation but the real labeled accuracy should be something in between these two if the parsing model have already seen this dependency type.

tested on	AS_U	AS_L	WW_U
Ery.(2008) Vo	76.0±0.2	67.0±0.3	82.7±0.5
Ery.(2008) Raw Data	73.3±0.3	63.2±0.3	80.6±0.7
Vo	76.1±0.2	67.4±0.3	83.0±0.2
Vd	74.7±0.2	63.3/66.5±0.3	81.8±0.2
Ve	75.5±0.2	66.7±0.3	82.5±0.2
Ve-o	74,0±0,2	62,4/65.7±0,3	81,1±0,1

Table 3: The parser's performance trained on the original treebank (Vo)

The fifth line of the Table 3 gives the results on the enlarged version of the treebank. We see that although the results are higher than Vd, they are not as good as Vo. From here, we understand that by collapsing some words into single units, we disappeared some of the dependencies where the parser was already very successful at finding; the average scores were getting higher by the success coming from this type of dependencies. As a final step in this set of experiments, we tested our parser on version Ve-o and saw that the results are worse than the results on the detached version (Vd): Collecting the new MWE components into single units gives worse results than doing no MWE processing at all. But is this just an illusion[8] or is there really a bad effect on the discovery of the remaining dependencies also? Actually the results provided here is not enough for answering this question. In order to see the exact picture we should examine the results more closely (Section 5.5).

5.4 Experiment Set II

In this set of experiments, we are looking at the results by using the new treebank versions in the training stage as well. Table 4 shows that in all of the test set combinations, the worst results are obtained by training with the enlarged treebank (Ve).

train.	test.	AS_U	AS_L	WW_U
Vo	Ve	75.5±0.2	66.7±0.3	82.5±0.2
	Vo	**76.1**±0.2	**67.4**±0.3	**83.0**±0.2
	Vd	**74.7**±0.2	**63.3**±0.3	**81.8**±0.2
Vd	Ve	75.3±0.2	65.9±0.3	82.4±0.2
	Vo	**76.0**±0.2	**66.7**±0.3	**82.9**±0.1
	Vd	**76.0**±0.2	**65.9**±0.3	**82.7**±0.2
Ve	Ve	75.3±0.2	66.7±0.3	82.3±0.2
	Vo	75,7±0.2	67,1±0.3	82,7±0.2
	Vd	74.3±0.2	63.0±0.3	81.4±0.2

Table 4: Parser's performance by training and testing with the different versions of the treebank

Table 4 shows that the results on the detached test set (Vd) are better when trained by Vd (76.0±0.2 AS_U) rather than the original treebank Vo (74.7±0.2 AS_U). This means that the parser is better at find-

[8] caused by the removed dependencies after the combination of the MWE constituents into single units in Ve-o: if the parser was already highly successful at finding these, the combination operation would certainly give the effect of a success decrease in the average.

ing the dependencies if it has samples from the same genre. But again by just looking the results this way, it is not possible to understand the situation entirely.

5.5 Experiment Set III

In order to be able to understand what is happening on the dependencies within MWEs and their surrounding structures, we are evaluating the results on 3 different ways described in Section 5.2. Table 5 gives the scores in all of thees three evaluation types; The first column block states each training and testing combination together with the number of combined MWEs and the total number of dependencies in the test sets. The second column block gives the overall results of the parser. The fourth column block lists the results obtained on the dependencies (with MWE label) occurring between the constituent words which appeared after the detachment of the MWEs annotated on the original treebank. The third column block gives the results obtained on the remaining dependencies (excluding the ones with MWE label). Example: The number of MWE labeled dependencies is 0 for the Vo and 2427 for Vd meaning that the detachment of 2040 combined MWEs (two or more words) on Vo resulted to 2427 dependencies. Thus, the average number of dependency per MWE is 1.19.

From the Table 5, we may now analyze the parser's performance in detail; We observe that the parser's performance (trained on the original treebank) drops significantly when it is tested on the detached version both on the overall results (76.1 $\rightarrow$ 74.7 AS_U) and excluding MWEs (76.1 $\rightarrow$ 75.9 AS_U, 83.0 $\rightarrow$ 82.8 WW_U the difference is small but statistically significant (McNemar $p<0.01$)). We see that the tests on Ve-o not only causes a decrease on the overall accuracy (74.7 $\rightarrow$ 74.0 AS_U) but also a decrease on the dependencies excluding MWEs (75.9 $\rightarrow$ 74.7 AS_U). Thus, we may say that the combination of MWEs listed in the dictionary has a harming effect on the determination of other syntactic structures as well. On the other side, we observe that the combination of MWEs annotated in the original treebank has a positive effect on the determination of other syntactic structures (from Vd to Vo the AS_U differs 75.9 $\rightarrow$ 76.1 but from Vd to Ve-o the AS_U differs 75.9 $\rightarrow$ 74.7).

These results bring the question: "What is the difference between the dictionary MWE list and the treebank MWE list?" In order to answer this question, we manually classified the MWEs in the Turkish treebank into six categories which are listed in Table 6. The second column in the table lists the number of MWEs in each categories, the third column lists the number of dependencies when we detach these MWEs and the fourth column gives the WW_U scores on the dependencies from these specific MWE categories. We only look at the WW_U scores since the IG-based links are created automatically and WW_U scores is considered to be more informative. The results are obtained with a parsing model trained with Version Vd. (it is obvious that a model trained with Vo won't be able to find most of these dependencies because of the lack of samples.)

MWE type	#of MWEs	#of Dep.	WW_U
Named ent.	618	941	83.7
Num. exp.	98	123	82.1
Comp. func.	54	54	5.6
Dup.	206	206	66.5
Comp. vn.	1061	1103	93.0

Table 6: Parser's success on special MWE types: Named Entities (Named ent.), Numerical Expressions (Num.exp.), Compound function words (Comp.func.), Duplications (Dup), Compound verb and noun formations (Comp.vn.)

We see from the Table 6, the parser is very bad (5.6 WW_U) at determining the compound function words (which are very rare) (Figure 3) and duplications[9] (66.5 WW_U). These dependencies could actually be easily discovered by a rule-based extractor. The success on named entities (83.7) and number expressions (82.1) could be considered as good but one shouldn't forget that the training and testing data is from the same treebank and the sentences could actually not be considered as random. Thus on a totally unseen data, these results would be lower. But again we believe a rule-based extractor for numerical and date expressions could be developed with

[9]"These are partial or full duplications of the forms involved and can actually be viewed as morphological derivational processes mediated by reduplication across multiple tokens." Oflazer et al. (2004) Example: "uyur uyumaz" ((he) sleeps (he) doesn't sleep) the MWE meaning is "as soon as (he) sleep".

train on	test on	# of comb. MWEs	# of Dep.	Overall results			Results Excl. MWE type dependencies(# of Dep= 43572)			Results on MWE type dependencies				
				AS_U	AS_L	WW_U	AS_U	AS_L	WW_U	# of Dep.	AS_U	P	R	WW_U
Vo	Vo	2040	43572	76.1±0.2	67.4±0.3	83.0±0.2	n/c	n/c	n/c	0	n/a	n/a	n/a	n/a
	Vd	0	45999	74.7±0.2	63.3/66.5±0.3	81.8±0.2	75.9±0.2	67,2±0.3	82.8±0.1	2427	62.1	n/a	n/a	73.1
	Ve	3674	41847	75.5±0.2	66.7±0.3	82.5±0.2	n/c	n/c	n/c	0	n/a	n/a	n/a	n/a
	Ve-o	1697	44217	74,0±0,2	62,4/65.7±0,3	81,1±0,1	74.7±0.2	65.9±0.3	81.7±0.2	2369	60.7	n/a	n/a	71.9
	S1	976	44675	75,6±0,2	65,4/67.2±0,3	82,8±0,1	76.0±0.2	67.3±0.3	83.0±0.2	1103	72.1	n/a	n/a	91.4
	S2	770	44881	75,4±0,2	65,1/67.0±0,3	82,6±0,1	76.0±0.2	67.3±0.3	82.9±0.2	1309	67.2	n/a	n/a	84.2
	S3	716	44935	75,2±0,2	64,9/66.9±0,3	82,4±0,1	75.9±0.2	67.2±0.3	82.8±0.1	1363	64.6	n/a	n/a	81.0
Vd	Vo	2040	43572	76.0±0.2	66.7±0.3	82.9±0.1	n/c	n/c	n/c	0	n/a	n/a	n/a	n/a
	Vd	0	45999	76.0±0.2	65.9/68.0±0.3	82.7±0.2	76.0±0.2	66.6±0.3	82.8±0.2	2427	81.6	71.3	57.2	86.2
	Ve	3674	41847	75.3±0.2	65.9±0.3	82.4±0.2	n/c	n/c	n/c	0	n/a	n/a	n/a	n/a
	Ve-o	1697	44217	75.2±0.2	65.1/67.0±0.3	82.0±0.2	74.9±0.2	65.7±0.3	81.9±0.2	2369	79.9	73.4	55.4	84.6
	S1	976	44675	**76.0**±0.2	66.2/67.8±0.3	**82.9**±0.2	**76.0**±0.2	66.6±0.3	**82.9**±0.2	1103	**85.6**	51.9	53.3	**93.0**
	S2	770	44881	75.9±0.2	66.1/67.8±0.3	82.8±0.2	76.0±0.2	66.7±0.3	82.9±0.2	1309	82.1	55.7	52.2	88.9
	S3	716	44935	75.8±0.2	65.9/67.7±0.3	82.6±0.1	76.0±0.2	66.6±0.3	82.9±0.2	1363	79.0	54.0	50.1	85.5

Table 5: Overall Parsing Results (on and outside MWEs) with different treebank versions:
n/c:no change with the previous results on the left column block (overall results); n/a:not available

high success. The best performance (93.0) of the parser is on the MWE of types compound verb and noun formations. We see that this is the class with the highest number of MWEs. And when we look at the dependencies on the dictionary list, we see that almost all of the MWEs are from this class; i.e. compound verb and noun formations. So actually by creating the enlarged version (Ve) of the treebank, we added 1697 more MWEs into this category where the parser is already very good at discovering. So what is going wrong when we combine these MWEs into single units in the preprocessing step? Instead of having an accuracy of 93% with automatic detection, we would have an accuracy of 100% with our deterministic approach. The problem is that when we do this we actually increase the lexical sparsity. For example, the verb "etmek" (to do) in Turkish may produce many MWEs such as "ikaz etmek" (to warn), "buyur etmek" (to welcome), "fark etmek" (to notice) and so on. And this is a very frequent verb in Turkish; it occurs 388 times in the current Turkish Treebank where in 340 of them it formed a MWE (already annotated in the treebank). With the addition of the dictionary list, 27 more MWEs constructed with "etmek" is added to the treebank. When we combine the MWEs constructed with this verb into single units we are actually splitting its frequency to many rarely occurring MWEs.

The next question is "If the addition of more MWEs of type compound verb and noun formations caused an accuracy decrease in parsing performance, could we obtain better or similar results by detaching the MWEs from this type and leaving the others as in the original?" If the answer is yes, then we could develop type specific MWE extractors according to the results. To answer our new question, we tested on 3 new versions of the treebank which consists the following subsets of MWEs:

- Subset 1 (S1)- Vo excluding MWEs of type compound verb and noun formations (meaning that only this type of MWEs are detached into their constituents and the others are left combined.)
- Subset 2 (S2)- S1 excluding MWEs of type duplications.
- Subset 3 (S3)- S2 excluding MWEs type compound function words.

Table 5 gives the results for the subsets as well. We see from the table that S1 has 1103 dependencies with MWE label (of type compound verb and noun formations). The unlabeled results of the tests on S1 are better than the tests on Vd, Ve, Ve-o and very close to the results on Vo. This means that, a MWE extractor concentrating only on the MWEs of type named entities, numerical expressions, duplications and some compound function words already annotated in the treebank could obtain similar results to the scores on the original treebank. But we see that we still have a problem with labeled accuracies. The addition of the new label increased the complexity for the parser and caused false positive assignments on dependencies from other types.

5.6 Experiment Set IV

To alleviate the problem observed in the labeled accuracy, instead of assigning the new "MWE" label to the detached MWEs, we developped a rule based dependency label chooser which assigns an appropriate label to these dependencies obeying the Turkish Treebank annotation approach. We have 16 rules similar to the following one:

if DEPENDENCY LABEL eq 'MWE'{
if HEAD's POSTAG eq 'Verb'
&& DEPENDENT's POSTAG eq 'Adverb'
then change MWE$\rightarrow$ MODIFIER
}

We changed the MWE labels in S1 and Vd by using this rule based dependency label chooser. Table 7 gives the results at the end of this operation.

train.	test.	AS_U	AS_L	WW_U
Vo	Vo	76.1±0.2	67.4±0.3	83.0±0.2
	Vd*	74.7±0.2	66.1±0.2	81.8±0.2
S1*	S1*	76.1±0.2	67.6±0.3	82.9±0.2
	Vd*	75.3±0.2	66.7±0.2	81.9±0.2

Table 7: Parsing results with MWE labels replaced by the label chooser

The results are as we expected. In the training stage, if we use our new version of the treebank (S1*) (where we detached the MWEs of type compound noun and verb formations) instead of the original one, the results on raw data (Vd*) (2nd and 4th lines of Table 7) became significantly better (AS_U and AS_L difference is statistically significant with McNemar ($p < 0.01$)). We also validated this outcome by testing on the validation set. Table 8 gives the results on both the original version of the validation set (ITU-Vo) and the detached version (ITU-Vd*). Although the small number of available MWEs (only 89), we observe an improvement by using the model trained with S1*. For the first two lines the improvement is rather small but statistically significant on labeled accuracy with Mcnemar($p<0.05$).

train.	test.	AS_U	AS_L	WW_U
Vo	ITU-Vo	80.42	72.47	84.55
S1*	ITU-Vo	81.01	73.25	84.68
Vo	ITU-Vd*	80.02	72.21	84.13
S1*	ITU-Vd*	80.65	72.94	84.32

Table 8: Results on Validation Set
(The trained model is on the data of 9 cross validation fold; the training set size is the same with other experiments)

Another outcome that could be observed from Table 7 (by comparing the first and third lines of results) is that a MWE extractor for only MWEs of types named entities, duplications, numbers, dates and some predefined list of compound prepositions would be enough for obtaining the results of the gold-standard treebank (there is no statistically significant results between these two lines). As a final comment, we may conclude that the preprocessing of the test data would improve the results by nearly 1.5 in IG-based evaluations (74.7→76.1, 66.1→67.6) and 1.1 (81.8→82.9) in word-based evaluation (2nd and 3rd lines of Table 7) if we also train with S1* instead of the original treebank. One should remember that there are in total 1324 fewer dependencies (Table 5) in S1 compared to Vd. These dependencies are expected to be discovered by the MWE extractor.

6 Conclusion

In this paper, we made a detailed analysis on multiword expression extraction on parsing accuracy of a statistical dependency parser. Our results showed that different MWE types have different impacts on the parser's performance. During the experiments, for the representation of MWEs in parsing data, we used a highly adopted strategy and combined the MWEs' constituents into single units. But we observed that when this approach is applied to the MWE types that could already be determined by the parser with a high success, the overall performance is decreased instead of increasing. The reason is mostly due to the lexical sparsity caused by the representation of the MWEs (as a single unit).

Although the development of a high accuracy MWE extractor was out of scope of this paper, during the analysis of different MWE types, we observed that most of them (which helped to increase parsing performance) could be easily found by creating rule-based MWE extractors. As the future work, we plan to develop such an extractor and evaluate the real parsing performance by using it. Another research topic will certainly be to investigate different MWE representations (others than the combination strategy).

Acknowledgments

The authors want to thank Mehmet Altıparmak for his help during the creation of the new treebank versions.

References

Sabine Buchholz and Erwin Marsi. 2006. Conll-X shared task on multilingual dependency parsing. In *Proceedings of the 10th Conference on Computational Natural Language Learning*, pages 149–164, New York, NY. Association for Computational Linguistics.

Conor Cafferkey. 2008. Exploiting multi-word units in statistical parsing and generation. Master's thesis, Dublin City University, Ireland.

Gülşen Eryiğit. 2007. ITU validation set for Metu-Sabancı Turkish treebank. March.

Gülşen Eryiğit, Joakim Nivre, and Kemal Oflazer. 2008. Dependency parsing of Turkish. *Computational Linguistics*, 34(3):357–389.

Deirdre Hogan, Jennifer Foster, and Josef van Genabith. 2011. Decreasing lexical data sparsity in statistical syntactic parsing - experiments with named entities. In *Proceedings of the Workshop on Multiword Expressions: from Parsing and Generation to the Real World*, pages 14–19, Portland, Oregon, USA, June. Association for Computational Linguistics.

Valia Kordoni, Carlos Ramisch, and Aline Villavicencio, editors. 2011. *Proceedings of the Workshop on Multiword Expressions: from Parsing and Generation to the Real World*. Association for Computational Linguistics, Portland, Oregon, USA, June.

Ioannis Korkontzelos and Suresh Manandhar. 2010. Can recognising multiword expressions improve shallow parsing? In *Human Language Technologies: The 2010 Annual Conference of the North American Chapter of the Association for Computational Linguistics*, pages 636–644, Los Angeles, California, June. Association for Computational Linguistics.

Jens Nilsson and Joakim Nivre. 2008. Malteval: An evaluation and visualization tool for dependency parsing. In *In Proceedings of the Sixth International Language Resources and Evaluation. LREC*.

Joakim Nivre and Jens Nilsson. 2004. Multiword units in syntactic parsing. In *MEMURA 2004 - Methodologies and Evaluation of Multiword Units in Real-World Applications, Workshop at LREC 2004*, pages 39–46, Lisbon, Portugal, May. In Dias, G., Lopes, J. G. P. and Vintar, S. (eds.).

Joakim Nivre, Johan Hall, Jens Nilsson, Gülşen Eryiğit, and Stetoslav Marinov. 2006. Labeled pseudo-projective dependency parsing with support vector machines. In *Proceedings of the 10th Conference on Computational Natural Language Learning*, pages 221–225, New York, NY.

Joakim Nivre, Johan Hall, Jens Nilsson, Atanas Chanev, Gülşen Eryiğit, Sandra Kübler, Stetoslav Marinov, and Erwin Marsi. 2007. Maltparser: A language-independent system for data-driven dependency parsing. *Natural Language Engineering Journal*, 13(2):99–135.

Kemal Oflazer, Bilge Say, Dilek Z. Hakkani-Tür, and Gökhan Tür. 2003. Building a Turkish treebank. In A. Abeillé, editor, *Treebanks: Building and Using Parsed Corpora*, pages 261–277. Kluwer, London.

Kemal Oflazer, Özlem Çetinoğlu, and Bilge Say. 2004. Integrating morphology with multi-word expression processing in Turkish. In Takaaki Tanaka, Aline Villavicencio, Francis Bond, and Anna Korhonen, editors, *Second ACL Workshop on Multiword Expressions: Integrating Processing*, pages 64–71, Barcelona, Spain, July. Association for Computational Linguistics.

Kemal Oflazer. 1994. Two-level description of Turkish morphology. *Literary and Linguistic Computing*, 9(2):137–148.

TDK. 2011. Turkish Language Association Turkish dictionary. `http://www.tdk.gov.tr`.

Linguistically Rich Graph Based Data Driven Parsing For Hindi

Samar Husain, Pujitha Gade and Rajeev Sangal
Language Technologies Research Centre, IIIT-Hyderabad, India.
{samar, pujitha.gade}@research.iiit.ac.in, sangal@mail.iiit.ac.in

Abstract

In this paper we show how linguistic knowledge can be incorporated during graph based parsing. We use MSTParser and show that the use of a constraint graph, instead of a complete graph, to extract a spanning tree improves parsing accuracy. A constraint graph is formed by using linguistic knowledge of a constraint based parsing system. Through a series of experiments we formulate the optimal constraint graph that gives us the best accuracy. These experiments show that some of the previous MSTParser errors can be corrected consistently. It also shows the limitations of the proposed approach.

1 Introduction

In MSTParser (McDonald et al., 2005a, 2005b; a graph based data driven parser), a complete graph is used to extract a spanning tree during derivation. MSTParser's learning model uses large-margin algorithm, which optimizes the parameters of the model to maximize the score margin between the correct dependency graph and all incorrect dependency graphs for every sentence in a training set. The learning procedure is global. Unlike, MaltParser (and other transition based systems, see Kubler et al., 2009), MSTParser considers limited history of parser decisions during training. McDonald and Nivre (2007) characterize in detail the specific error patterns in MSTParser. Recent works such as Sagae and Lavie (2006), Nivre and McDonald (2008), Zhang and Clark (2008), Koo and Collins (2010), have tried to improve the parsing accuracy either by integrating the two parsers via stacking, etc. or by introducing better learning models.

In this work we try to investigate if parsing accuracy using MSTParser can be improved by providing it a constraint graph instead of a complete graph during the derivation step. Our work is related to Bergsma and Cherry, (2010), where they try something similar to increase parser speed. We modify the Chu-Liu-Edmonds algorithm such that it would start with the modified graph instead of a complete graph. This algorithm was chosen over the Eisner's algorithm as the Hindi treebank contains ~14% non-projective arcs (Mannem et al., 2009). While we do not change the learning phase, it will be interesting to see what effect certain linguistic knowledge alone can have on the overall accuracy. A constraint graph is formed by using linguistic knowledge of a constraint based parsing system (Bharati et al., 2009). Through a series of experiments we formulate the optimal constraint graph that gives us the best accuracy. These experiments show that some of the previous MSTParser errors can be corrected consistently. It also shows the limitations of the proposed approach.

The paper is arranged as follows, in section 2 we briefly discuss the notion of a constraint graph for a sentence; Section 3 describes the experimental setup. The experiments are discussed in section 4, followed by the results and observations in section 5. We finally conclude the paper along with future directions in section 6.

2 Constraint Graph

Bharati et al., (2009) proposed a two-stage constraint based hybrid dependency parsing approach for free word order languages. They divide the task of parsing into intra-clausal and inter-clausal stages. At each stage valency frames for various heads (mainly for verbs and conjunctions) are used to construct a constraint graph. The parser currently uses close to 536 manually annotated valency frames. The constraint graph is then converted into an integer programming problem to get the parse at each stage. Let us look at a sample constraint graph for a Hindi sentence.

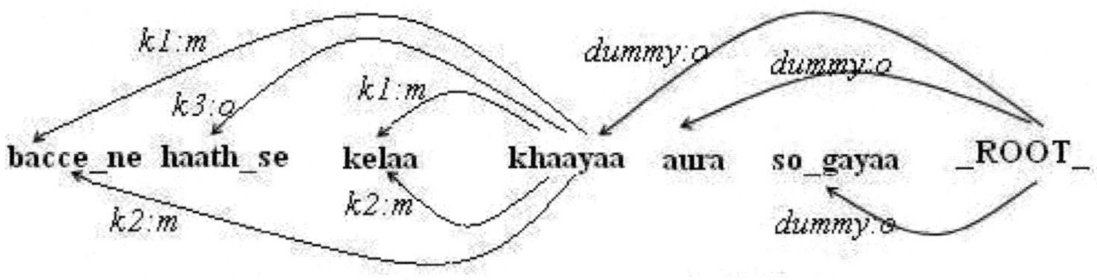

(a) 1st stage Constraint Graph

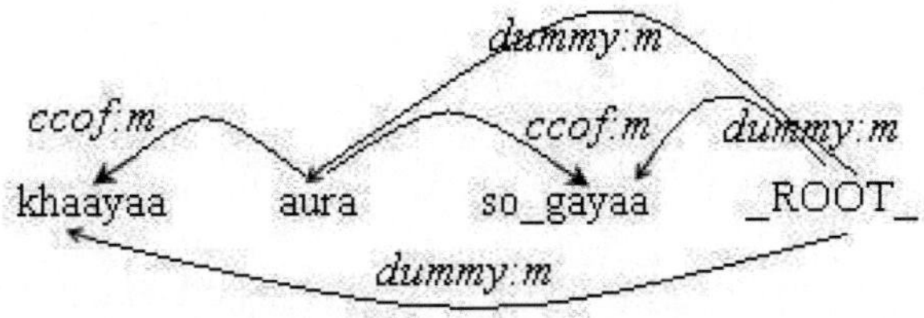

(b) 2nd stage Constraint Graph

Figure 1. Constraint graph for sentence 1.
(Although a constraint graph has arc labels, they are not used in our experiments.)

(1) *bacce ne haath_se kelaa khaayaa*
'child' ERG hand_with 'banana' 'eat'
aura so gayaa
'and' 'sleep' PAST
'The child ate the banana with his hand and slept'

Figure 1 shows the 1st stage and the 2nd stage Constraint graph (CG) for Example 1. Note that the arcs in 1st stage CG are localized to individual clauses. The _ROOT_ node is required in order to get the partial parse at the end of the 1st stage. Also note that in the 2nd stage only the inter-clausal relations are considered (here finite verbs and a conjunctions). In such a scenario 1st stage and 2nd stage CGs are distinct and vary drastically in size. This can be clearly seen in Figure 1.

The CG for each sentence provides the linguistic knowledge that we will use in various experiments in this paper. We can use this information in two ways:

a) Complete CG or stage specific CG can be directly used instead of a complete graph during the derivation.
b) Specific information from CG can be used to prune out certain arcs in the complete graph while retaining others.

For the experiments discussed in this paper we use the latter. We note that although CG also provides arc labels, for all our experiments we are only concerned with the attachment information. This is because the spanning tree extraction algorithm in MSTParser uses unlabeled graph. MSTParser uses a separate classifier to label the trees.

3 Experimental Setup

All the experiments are conducted on Hindi. We use the dependency treebank released as part of the ICON2010 tools contest (Husain et al., 2010). The training data had 2,973 sentences. Development and testing had 543 and 321 sentences respectively. MSTParser[1] was modified so that it can use CG during derivation. We use the non-projective algorithm, order=1 and training k=5. We use the feature set optimized for Hindi by Bharati et al. (2008). Experiments were first conducted using training and development data. Once the experimental design was frozen, only then the test data was used.

4 Experiments

For an input $S = w_0, w_1, \ldots w_n$, i.e. the set of all words in a sentence, let G_S be the complete graph, and CG_S be the constraint graph provided by the constraint parser. Let $N = \{w_0, w_1, \ldots w_n\}$ be the

[1] MST Version 0.4b

set of vertices in G_S. A_G = N x N and $A_{CG} \subseteq$ N x N is the set of arcs in the two graphs. An arc between w_i and w_j, shown as (w_i,w_j) signifies w_i as the parent of w_j. X is the set of all the nodes which occurs as a child in A_{CG}. Also, let C be the set of all vertices which are conjunctions, V be the set of all vertices which are verbs, K be the set of all vertices which are nouns, P be the set of all vertices that have a case-marker/post-position and J be the set of adjectives.

The set of arcs which will be pruned from the complete graph in experiment 1 is shown in Table 1. This means that all the arcs in G will be pruned except the ones present in CG.

```
For y in X:
    For x in S:
        If ∄ (x,y) in A_CG:
            Remove (x,y) from A_G
```

Table1. Experiment 1 valid arcs

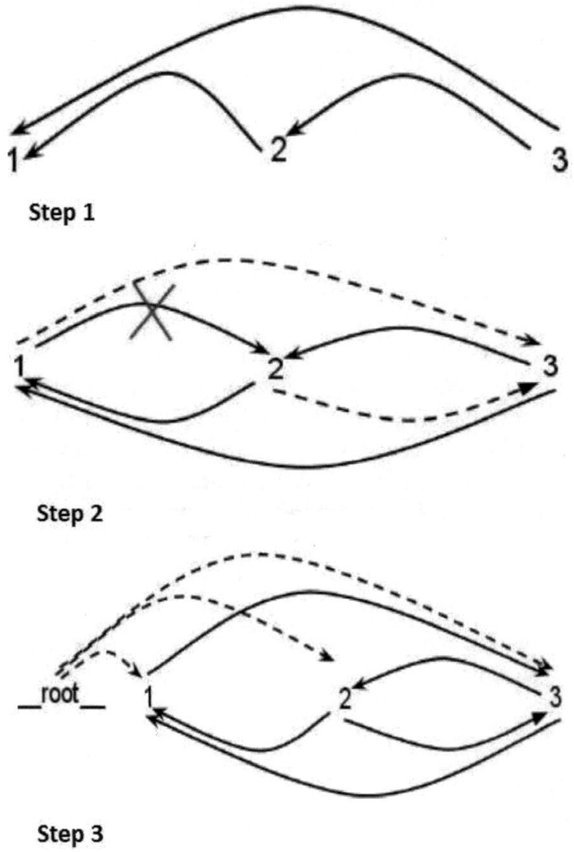

Figure 2. Illustration of Experiment 1

Experiment 1 is illustrated in Figure 2. Step 1 is a sample constraint graph for a sentence with three words which are represented as 1, 2 and 3. In step 2 we prune arcs according to the Constraint graph. For nodes which have no parents in CG we keep all their incoming arcs intact as shown in Figure 2 with dashed arcs. In step 3 we add arcs from __ROOT__ to all the nodes. The final graph is used by MSTParser to extract the parse tree during derivation.

The parser in experiment 1 (E1) outperformed the baseline UAS (more details in section 5). Further analysis showed that the pruning based on E1, although useful, also had some negative effect, i.e. it also prunes out many potentially valid arcs that would have been originally considered by MSTParser. Through experiments 2-8 we explore if we can minimize such invalid pruning. We do this by systematically considering parts of the CG and using only those parts for pruning G.

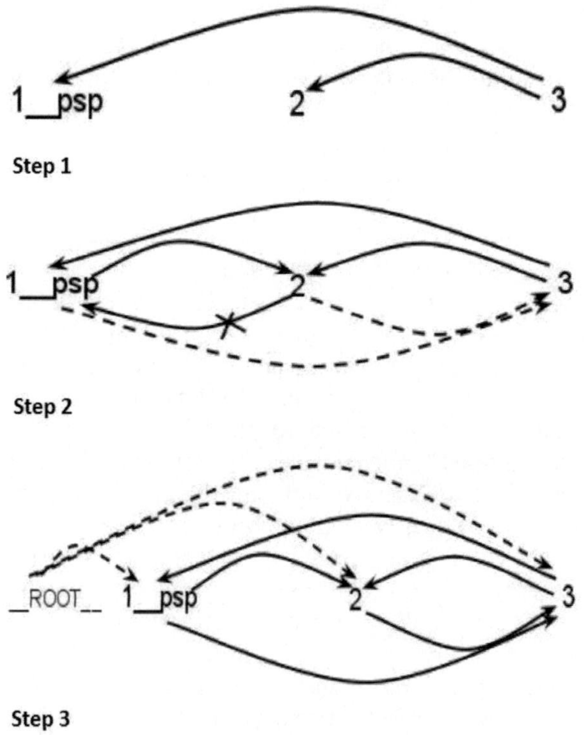

Figure 3. Illustration of Experiment 2

Experiment 2 (Table 2, 1st row) begins with focusing on child nodes with post-positions. Also incorporated are the conjunction heads. Since a CG is formed based on explicit linguistic cues, it makes sense to base our decision where concrete information is available. Experiment 2 is illustrated in Figure 3. Experiment 3 (Table 2, 2nd row) uses similar conditions, except the constraint of nodes with post-position is only on noun children. By doing this we are trying to explore the most appropriate information in the CG.

```
For y in X:
    For x in S:
        If ∄ (x,y) in A_CG:
            Remove (x,y) from A_G
        If ∃ (x,y) in A_CG and y∉P and x∉C:
            Remove(x,y) from A_G
```

```
For y in X:
    For x in S:
        If ∄ (x,y) in A_CG:
            Remove (x,y) from A_G
        If ∃ (x,y) in A_CG and y∈K and y∉P and x∉C:
            Remove(x,y) from A_G
```

Table 2. Experiment 2 and 3 valid arcs

```
For y in X:
    For x in S:
        If ∄ (x,y) in A_CG:
            Remove (x,y) from A_G
        If ∃ (x,y) in A_CG and y∈K and y∉P and x∈V:
            Remove(x,y) from A_G
```

Table 3. Experiment 4 valid arcs

It is interesting to note that in experiment 4 we are trying to prune out invalid arcs related to the argument structure information of a verb ($x \in V$) available in a CG. Using CG only for verbal arguments with case-marker captures various verbal alternations manifested via case-markings.

Experiment 5 and 6 extends experiments 4 and 3 respectively by introducing an exception where a noun child *y* with no case-marker is considered only if there exists other potential conjunction/adjectival head for *y*. Owing to the free-word order property of Hindi, identifying the head of a noun with no case-marker is a rather difficult task. In spite of their availability many robust generalizations (that help disambiguate relations with nouns with no case-markings) such as agreement remain unexploited during training (Ambati et al., 2010). In this experiment therefore, we are trying to ensure that the ambiguity of correct heads for nouns with no post-position is not resolved by CG.

```
For y in X:
    For x in S:
        If ∄ (x,y) in A_CG:
            Remove (x,y) from A_G
        If ∃ (x,y) in A_CG and y∈K and y∉P and x∈V:
            If ∄ (z,y) in A_CG and (z∈C or z∈J)
                Remove(x,y) from A_G
```

```
For y in X:
    For x in S:
        If ∄ (x,y) in A_CG:
            Remove (x,y) from A_G
        If ∃(x,y) in A_CG and y∈K and y∉P and x∉C:
            If ∄ (z,y) in A_CG and (z∈C or z∈J)
                Remove(x,y) from A_G
```

Table 4. Experiment 5 and 6 valid arcs

Experiments 2-6 only catered to verbal, conjunction or adjectival head. Experiment 7 and 8 extend 5 and 6 to handle nominal predicate heads. We note here that this information is not obtained from the CG and is being treated as a heuristic rather than having some linguistic validity. The constraint parser has very limited coverage for nominal predicates and therefore we cannot rely on it for this kind of information. The heuristic considers a possibility of an attachment between two consecutive nouns and does not remove such arcs from the G.

5 Results and Discussion

Figure 4 shows the results for all the experiment. The baseline UAS was 88.66 and the best result was obtained from experiment 8 with the UAS of 89.31. This is an increase of 0.65%. There was also an increase of 0.45% in the LAS. All the improvements in the results were statistically significant using McNemar's test ($p<0.01$ for improvement in UAS).

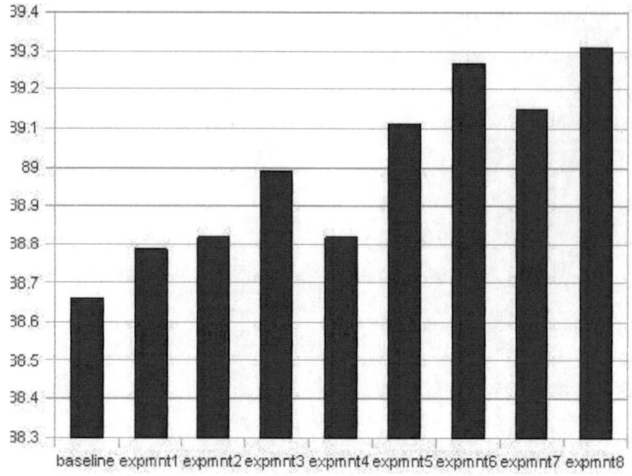

Figure 4. UAS of all the experiments.

Table 5 shows that the improvement in the accuracies is spread across different kinds of relations.

Relations	Baseline		Experiment 8	
	UAS	LAS	UAS	LAS
Intra-clausal	87.86	73.63	88.30	74.00
Verbal Args* (Intra-clausal)	89.46	72.28	90.02	72.68
Non-args (Intra-clausal)	86.25	75.00	86.57	75.32
Inter-clausal	91.85	91.53	93.29	92.33

Table 5. Comparison of baseline and Experiment 8 accuracies for various relations.
(*Args: arguments)

Both inter-clausal as well as intra-clausal relations benefit. Within a clause, both argument structure of a verb and other relations are better identified in Experiment 8 when compared to the baseline. There was a consistent improvement in the analysis of certain phenomenon. These were:

a) Intra-clausal coordinating conjunction as dependents. These may appear either as arguments of the verb or as children of non-verbal heads.
b) Better handling of arguments of non-finite verbs and gerunds
c) Better handling of clausal arguments and relative clauses.

A similar pattern is seen from Table 6 where there is an increase for almost all the POS tags in the head attachment accuracy, except for adjectival attachments.

As mentioned earlier, the constraint graph is originally formed using the linguistic knowledge of the constraint based system. It is clear that for our experiments the coverage of this knowledge is very crucial. Our experiments show that while the coverage of verbal and conjunction heads is good, knowledge of other heads such as predicative nouns and adjectives is lacking. As mentioned earlier the constraint parser currently uses close to 536 valence frames. It would be interesting to see how grammar extraction methods for Hindi (Kolachina et al., 2010) can be combined with our approach to boost the knowledge base being currently used.

POS tag	%Instance	Accuracy	
		Baseline	E8
Noun	64%	89%	90%
Finite verb	15%	94%	95%
Non-finite verb	3%	83%	83%
Gerund	5%	86%	88%
Conjunction	7%	75%	77%
Adjective	4%	98%	95%

Table 6. Head attachment accuracy distribution over POS

6 Conclusion and Future directions

In this paper we successfully integrated linguistically driven constraint graph in MSTParser. Through a series of experiments we showed that selective use of such information leads to improvement in parser accuracy. Through analyzing the results we fleshed out the areas of improvement. We also pointed out where our approach harms the parsing accuracy.

The linguistic knowledge in all our experiments are currently being used as hard constraints, but they can also be used as soft constraints similar to parser stacking approaches explored by Nivre and McDonald, (2008) and Husain et al., (2011). Use of grammar extraction techniques in the future to automatically construct the constraint graph seems to present a very attractive strategy which can complement these experiments.

Acknowledgement

We would like to thank the three anonymous reviewers for their extensive and insightful comments that helped us improve the paper.

References

B. R. Ambati, S. Husain, J. Nivre and R. Sangal. 2010. On the Role of Morphosyntactic Features in Hindi Dependency Parsing. *In Proceedings of NAACL-HLT 2010 workshop on Statistical Parsing of Morphologically Rich Languages (SPMRL 2010), Los Angeles, CA.*

A. Bharati, S. Husain, D. M. Sharma and R. Sangal. 2009. Two stage constraint based hybrid approach to free word order language dependency parsing. *In Proceedings of the 11th International Conference on Parsing Technologies (IWPT). Paris.*

A. Bharati, S. Husain, B. Ambati, S. Jain, D. M. Sharma and R. Sangal. 2008. Two semantic features make all the difference in Parsing accuracy. *In Proceedings of the 6th International Conference on Natural Language Processing (ICON-08), CDAC Pune, India.*

S. Husain, P. Gadde, J. Nivre and R. Sangal. 2011. Clausal parsing helps data-driven dependency parsing: Experiments with Hindi. *In Proceedings of IJCNLP 2011.*

S. Husain, P. Mannem, B. R. Ambati, and P. Gadde. 2010. The ICON-2010 Tools Contest on Indian Language Dependency Parsing. *In Proceedings of ICON-2010 Tools Contest on Indian Language Dependency Parsing. Kharagpur, India.*

P. Kolachina, S. Kolachina, A. K. Singh, V. Naidu, S. Husain, R. Sangal and A. Bharati. 2010. Grammar Extraction from Treebanks for Hindi and Telugu. *In Proceedings of The 7th International Conference on Language Resources and Evaluation (LREC). Valleta. Malta. 2010.*

T. Koo and M. Collins. 2010. Efficient Third-order Dependency Parsers. In *Proc of ACL2010.*

S. Kubler, R. McDonald and J. Nivre. 2009. *Dependency parsing.* Morgan and Claypool.

P. Mannem, H. Chaudhry and A.Bharati. 2009. Insights into Non-projectivity in Hindi. *Proceedings of ACL-IJCNLP Student Research Workshop. Singapore.*

R. McDonald, K. Crammer, and F. Pereira. 2005a. Online large-margin training of dependency parsers. In *Proceedings of ACL 2005*. pp. 91–98.

R. McDonald, F. Pereira, K. Ribarov, and J. Hajic. 2005b. Non-projective dependency parsing using spanning tree algorithms. *Proceedings of HLT/EMNLP*, pp. 523–530.

R. McDonald and J. Nivre. 2007. Characterizing the Errors of Data-Driven Dependency Parsing Models. In *Proc of Joint Conference on Empirical Methods in Natural Language Processing and Computational Natural Language Learning*

J. Nilsson and J. Nivre. 2008. Malteval: An evaluation and visualization tool for dependency parsing. In t*he Proc of Sixth International Language Resources and Evaluation,* Marrakech, Morocco.

J. Nivre and R. McDonald. 2008. Integrating graph-based and transition-based dependency parsers. In *Proc. of ACL-HLT.*

J. Nivre. 2006. *Inductive Dependency Parsing*. Springer.

K. Sagae and A. Lavie. 2006. Parser combination by reparsing. In Proc. HLT/NAACL.

S. Bergsma and C. Cherry. 2010. Fast and Accurate Arc Filtering for Dependency Parsing. In *Proceedings of the 23rd International Conference on Computational Linguistics (Coling 2010).*

Y. Zhang and S. Clark. 2008. A tale of two parsers: Investigating and combining graph-based and transition-based dependency parsing. *In Proceedings of the Conference on Empirical Methods in Natural Language Processing (EMNLP), pages 562-571.*

Data point selection for self-training

Ines Rehbein
SFB 632: Information structure
University of Potsdam
irehbein@uni-potsdam.de

Abstract

Problems for parsing morphologically rich languages are, amongst others, caused by the higher variability in structure due to less rigid word order constraints and by the higher number of different lexical forms. Both properties can result in sparse data problems for statistical parsing. We present a simple approach for addressing these issues. Our approach makes use of self-training on instances selected with regard to their similarity to the annotated data. Our similarity measure is based on the perplexity of part-of-speech trigrams of new instances measured against the annotated training data. Preliminary results show that our method outperforms a self-training setting where instances are simply selected by order of occurrence in the corpus and argue that self-training is a cheap and effective method for improving parsing accuracy for morphologically rich languages.

1 Introduction

Up to now, most work on statistical parsing has been focussed on English, a language with a configurational word order and little morphology. The inherent properties of morphologically rich languages include a higher variability in structure due to less rigid word order constraints, thus leading to greater attachment ambiguities, and a higher number of different word forms, leading to coverage problems caused by sparse data. These issues pose a great challenge to statistical parsing.

One sensible way to treat these issues is the development of more sophisticated parsing models adapted to the language-specific properties of morphologically rich languages. Another, simpler approach, tries to overcome the problems outlined above by expanding the training data. Possible approaches for expansion include self-training and active learning.

For self-training a parser is trained on a seed dataset of gold trees and applied to new text, either coming from the same domain or, in the context of domain adaptation, from a domain different from the seed data. The parser output trees are then added to the seed data and the parser is re-trained on its own output. For the in-domain setting it is quite unintuitive why this approach should work, as we only add more of what the parser already knows, and we also include a considerable amount of errors in the training set.

Active learning, on the other hand, tries to expand the training set by selecting those instances which provide the parser with a high amount of new information.[1] The underlying idea is that those instances have yet to be learned by the parser and thus will support the learning process. These instances have to be labelled by a human coder (often called the oracle) and then added to the seed data. The parser is re-trained and new instances can be selected, based on the new model. The intuition why this approach should work is more straightforward than for the self-training setting: we do provide the model with new, unseen information and, assuming that our oracle is right, the amount of noise is kept to a minimum. The great advantage of self-training, however,

[1]Common measures for data point selection are based on the uncertainty of the model with regard to its own predictions.

is that it is unsupervised, thus obviating the need for human annotation.

In this study we test the potential of self-training for parsing morphologically rich languages. We present experiments for German, a language with rich morphology (relative to English) and semi-free word order, and show that self-training can improve parsing accuracy when only a small amount of labelled training data is available. Furthermore, we show that selecting sentences for self-training on the basis of similarity to the training data is a good strategy which can further improve results while avoiding the downside of expensive human annotation.

The paper is structured as follows. Section 2 reports on related work. Section 3 describes the setup of our experiments and reports preliminary results. In Section 4 we conclude and outline future work.

2 Related work

The question whether or not self-training can be employed to improve parsing accuracy and to overcome sparse data problems has gained a lot of attention in recent years. While training a generative parsing model on its own output (Charniak, 1997; Steedman et al., 2003) does not seem to work well, McClosky et al. (2006a; 2006b) showed promising results when combining the self-training approach with a two-stage reranking parser model (Charniak and Johnson, 2005). This triggered a number of follow-up studies especially in the area of domain adaptation (Bacchiani et al., 2006; Foster et al., 2007; McClosky et al., 2010), where self-training is used to adapt the parser to a target domain for which no (or only a small amount of) annotated training data is available.

(Reichart and Rappoport, 2007) are the first to report successful self-training using a generative parsing model only. They claim that the crucial difference to earlier studies is the size of the seed data and the number of parser output trees added to the training data. In their experiments they train a reimplementation of Collins' parsing model 2 on a small seed set of trees (100-2000 trees) from the WSJ and add automatically parsed analyses for WSJ sections 2-21. Then they test their models on section 23 of the WSJ and report a substantial improvement for the in-domain self-training setting.

Discussion has focussed on the question of which factors are responsible for the success (or failure) of self-training. Reichart and Rappoport (2007) show that the number of unknown words is a good indicator of the usefulness of self-training when applied to small seed data sets. McClosky et al. (2008) have provided a thorough analysis and conclude that an important source of improvement comes from seeing words already known to the parser in new contexts. A question which, until now, has not gained much attention is the impact of language-specific features on the effect of self-training.

Another strand of research related to our work is that of cross-language adaptation of parsers, where there exists labelled data for one language but none (or only little) for the other. Zeman and Resnik (2008) present cross-language adaptation of a constituency parser by mapping the part-of-speech tags from the source and target languages into a universal tagset, claiming that the similarities between two closely related languages allow for abstraction from the level of word forms. They apply their method to Danish and Swedish, two closely related languages, and present an f-score of 66.4% for constituency trees for Swedish after having trained their parser on data from the Danish treebank.

Søgaard (2011) pushes this line of research further and applies it to languages as different as Arabic, Bulgarian, Danish and Portuguese. The basic approach is similar to (Zeman and Resnik, 2008). Søgaard (2011) delexicalises the treebanks and maps the part-of-speech tags into one common tagset. Crucial for the success of his approach is the filtering of the training data. Søgaard only trains on the 90% of the source trees which are most similar to the target language. As a similarity measure he uses perplexity on the basis of POS ngrams. The results are quite impressive. Despite the very different properties of the languages Søgaard achieves f-scores in the range of 50-75% on full-length sentences.

We take up the idea of data point selection based on similarity and apply it to our self-training scenario. Is is not straightforward whether this strategy will work or not, as it may seem to be diametrically opposed to the idea of active learning, where the system is provided with instances with a high information content. Here, on the contrary, we select instances which are similar to the training data, which might mean that they do not contribute new, useful information for the parser. Nevertheless, we hope that, since they are similar to what the parser already knows, it might handle these instances reasonably well and therefore the amount of noise added to the training set will be small. At the same time we assume with McClosky et al. (2008) that one important factor in self-training is providing the parser with additional context for already known words, and therefore presume that selecting similar sentences will support the learning process.

3 Self-training experiments

3.1 Data

In our experiments we use data from two German treebanks. We take syntactically annotated trees from the TiGer treebank (Brants et al., 2002) and raw text from the TüBa-D/Z treebank (Telljohann et al., 2005). The TüBa-D/Z (Release 6) consists of 55 814 sentences, TiGer (Release 2) includes 50 474 sentences. Sentence length in the two treebanks is comparable, with around 17 words per sentence. TiGer is annotated with phrase structure trees, dependency (grammatical relation) information and POS tags, according to the Stuttgart Tübingen Tag Set (STTS) (Schiller et al., 1995). The tree structure is flat and does not contain unary nodes as non-local dependencies are encoded by the use of crossing branches.

Both treebanks include German newspaper text, coming from two different newspapers (Frankfurter Rundschau and *taz*). Rehbein and van Genabith (2007) showed that there are considerable domain differences between the two treebanks and that the texts can easily be separated on the basis of the distribution of part-of-speech tags in the two corpora.

3.2 Preprocessing

We use the TiGer trees as our training data and the sentences in the TüBa-D/Z for expanding the corpus. Our setup is as follows.

First we normalised different forms of apostrophes in the text.[2] Then we divided the 50474 trees in TiGer into training and test set, following the proposal described in Dubey (2004). We split the data into 20 buckets by placing the first tree of the treebank into bucket 1, the second tree into bucket 2, and so on. We then combined the content of buckets 1 to 19 into the training set (47951 trees), and used bucket 20 as our test set (2523 trees).

From the randomly ordered training set we created 8 new training subsets of increasing size, putting the first 5000 trees in the training set in subset 1, the first 10000 trees in subset 2, and so on, up to 40000 trees (subset 8). We resolved the crossing branches in the TiGer trees by attaching the non-head child nodes higher up in the tree, following (Kübler, 2005).

3.3 Data point selection

In the next step we created language models for each of the 8 TiGer training subsets on the basis of the part-of-speech trigrams[3] and computed the perplexity for each sentence in the TüBa-D/Z treebank based on its part-of-speech trigrams. The TüBa-D/Z POS tags used in our experiments have been assigned using the RFTagger (Schmid and Laws, 2008). For TiGer, we used the gold POS tags.

Perplexity (Equation 1) is an information-theoretic measure and can be used to assess the homogeneity of a corpus. It can be unpacked as the inverse of the corpus probability, normalised by corpus size. The perplexity of a sentence from the TüBa-D/Z tells us how similar this sentence is to the TiGer training data.

$$PP(W) = \sqrt[N]{\frac{1}{P(w_1 w_2 ... w_N)}} \qquad (1)$$

For each of the 8 subsets we selected the 25000 sentences from the TüBa-D/Z with the lowest perplexity, thus the TüBa-D/Z sentences most similar in structure to the respective TiGer training subset. Then we parsed the selected sentences and added them to the TiGer training data (subsets 1-8). We re-trained the parser and evaluated against the TiGer test set, comparing the results against the perfor-

[2] TiGer uses “ and ‘ for opening and ” and ’ for closing double quotes, TüBa-D/Z uses ‘ for opening and ’ for closing single quotes but does not distinguish between opening and closing double quotes.

[3] The language models were produced and calculated using the CMU/Cambridge toolkit (`http://mi.eng.cam.ac.uk/prc14/toolkit.html`).

mance of the parser when trained on the original subset from the TiGer treebank.

3.4 Parsing experiments

For our experiments we use the unlexicalised Berkeley parser (Petrov et al., 2006) and the lexicalised form of the Stanford parser (Klein and Manning, 2003). The Berkeley parser is an unlexicalised latent variable PCFG parser which uses a split-and-merge technique to automatically refine the training data. The splits result in more and more fine-grained subcategories, which are merged again if not proven useful. We train a PCFG from each of the 8 training subsets by carrying out six cycles of the split-and-merge process. The model is language-agnostic. The Stanford parser provides a factored probabilistic model combining a PCFG with a dependency model. We use the Stanford parser in its lexicalised, markovised form.[4]

Both parsers were trained on the syntactic nodes of the trees only, stripping off the grammatical function (GF) labels from the trees. We add the GF to the parser output in a postprocessing step, using the method of (Seeker et al., 2010), and include GF in the evaluation. Training the parser on syntactic node labels without GF has the advantage of considerably reducing the number of atomic labels in the grammar. As a result, we obtain smaller grammars which are more efficient for parsing, and we also avoid sparse data problems. We also lose information, but the treebank refinement techniques used by the Berkeley parser easily recover this information and thus yield comparable results for both settings. As an additional benefit we avoid the problem of multiple governable GF assigned to children of the same parent node, an error occasionally made by the Berkeley parser. The method by (Seeker et al., 2010), on the other hand, uses linguistically informed hard constraints to prevent these errors.

While we computed perplexity on the basis of the gold POS tags in TiGer treebank and automatically assigned POS tags to the TüBa-D/Z sentences, for parsing we used raw text as input and let the parsers assign their own POS tags.

[4]Parameters: `hmarkov=1, vmarkov=2`

3.5 Results

We compare the impact of self-training on parsing accuracy for a lexicalised (Stanford) and an unlexicalised (Berkeley) parsing model. For self-training we test the following settings: a) selecting new training data from TüBa-D/Z based on perplexity, adding the 25 000 parser output trees most similar to the TiGer training subset (PERPLEXITY) and b) adding the first 25 000 sentences from the TüBa-D/Z (FIRST) to each of the TiGer training subsets.

Table 1 shows results for the different settings including GF in the evaluation.[5] In general, the results for the Berkeley parser are much higher (according to the PARSEVAL metric) than the results for the lexicalised version of the Stanford parser. The most striking finding is that for the Stanford parser self-training was not able to improve parsing accuracy over the baseline of training the parser on the (much smaller) TiGer training subsets only, while for the Berkeley parser we get a significant improvement of 2.9% and 1.9% f-score for the two smallest training subsets. With increasing size of the training set the gap between the results achieved on the original TiGer training data and on the expanded training sets becomes smaller, but even for the largest training set we achieve a significant improvement of 0.9%.

While results for the Stanford parser are much lower than the ones for Berkeley and self-training fails to outperform the baseline in all cases, the general trend for the self-training settings (PERPLEXITY, FIRST) is the same. Selecting new training instances on the basis of similarity helps mostly for smaller data sets, while for the larger training sets there does not seem to be a significant difference between the two settings. This finding is quite intuitive. In the self-training setting we have a trade-off between new information provided to the parser and noise added to the training set. For small training sets new context information has a far higher impact, while for training sets of increasing size we already have more information in the labelled data, and thus the gains from providing additional context to the parser are lower than the harm we cause by

[5]For significance testing we use the Randomized Parsing Evaluation Comparator provided by Dan Bikel (`http://www.cis.upenn.edu/~dbikel/software.html#comparator`)

subset	5000	10000	15000	20000	25000	30000	35000	40000
		Stanford parser (BASELINE)						
precision	57.77***	62.22***	64.32***	65.57***	66.18***	66.38***	67.34***	68.13***
recall	61.24 .	64.37***	65.85***	66.81***	67.17***	76.29***	68.07***	68.81***
f-score	**59.46**	**63.27**	**65.08**	**66.18**	**66.67**	**66.84**	**67.70**	**68.40**
		Stanford parser, self-trained (PERPLEXITY)						
precision	55.02	59.89	62.43	63.20	63.82	64.86	65.61	66.53
recall	60.57	63.38	64.94	65.28	65.61	66.33	66.81	67.62
f-score	57.66	61.59	63.66	64.22	64.70	65.58	66.20	67.02
		Stanford parser, self-trained (FIRST)						
precision	54.60	59.89	62.42	63.34	64.36	64.93	65.94	66.75
recall	60.20	63.52	64.85	65.42	66.11	66.49	67.17	67.86
f-score	57.26	61.65	63.61	64.36	65.22	65.70	66.55	67.30
		Berkeley parser (BASELINE)						
precision	63.39	66.65	69.16	70.50	71.03	72.54	72.79	73.06
recall	63.22	66.50	68.88	70.07	70.72	72.11	72.41	72.71
f-score	63.30	66.58	69.02	70.28	70.87	72.32	72.60	72.88
		Berkeley parser, self-trained (PERPLEXITY)						
precision	66.39***	68.66***	70.23**	71.42**	71.55	73.59***	73.44 .	74.08***
recall	65.98***	68.43***	69.82**	71.05**	71.02	73.10***	72.74	73.55**
f-score	**66.18**	**68.54**	**70.02**	**71.23**	**71.28**	**73.34**	**73.09**	**73.82**
		Berkeley parser, self-trained (FIRST)						
precision	65.79***	68.20***	70.15**	71.02	71.03	72.23	73.20	73.21
recall	65.46***	67.69***	69.71*	70.47	70.72	71.82	72.55	72.71
f-score	65.63	67.94	69.93	70.74	70.87	72.03	72.88	72.96

Table 1: Parsing results (PARSEVAL) for the different self-training settings, including GF in the evaluation (asterisks indicate significant differences between self-training and the baseline: p=0.001***, p=0.005**, p=0.01*, p=0.05 .)

including erroneous parser output trees.

So far, it is not clear to us why the lexicalised parser performs poorly in the self-training setting. This result is in line with (Huang and Harper, 2009), who observed that the PCFG-LA parser used in their experiments benefitted more from self-training as compared to a lexicalised generative parser. However, our results are not necessarily an effect of lexicalisation, but might be due to the overall lower accuracy of the Stanford parser on German (see Kübler (2008)). A quantiative and qualitative error analysis might give us some interesting insight into the underlying reasons and into the question when and why self-training will work for parsing.

4 Conclusions and future work

We presented preliminary results on self-training experiments for German, a language with rich morphology and semi-free word order. We proposed a new approach to self-training where we select new instances on the basis of similarity to the seed training data. Our results show that this strategy helps to boost self-training results especially for small seed data, but also obtains a significant improvement for larger training sets.

Our approach offers plenty of room for improvement. In future work we plan to investigate the adequacy of different similarity measures for self-training, and also to measure similarity on different levels (so far we have only considered the part-of-speech level). An obvious extension is the integration of a reranker in order to add a different view on the selection process. We expect that this will have a positive impact on our results.

Finally, we plan to have a closer look at the impact of language-specific properties on self-training. Our intuition is that the potential of self-training might be larger for morphologically rich languages, but this claim has yet to be tested.

Acknowledgments

We would like to thank the anonymous reviewers for their helpful comments and suggestions.

References

Michiel Bacchiani, Michael Riley, Brian Roark, and Richard Sproat. 2006. Map adaptation of stochastic grammars. *Computer Speech and Language*, 20.

Sabine Brants, Stefanie Dipper, Silvia Hansen, Wolfgang Lezius, and George Smith. 2002. The TIGER treebank. In *Proceedings of the First Workshop on Treebanks and Linguistic Theories*.

Eugene Charniak and Mark Johnson. 2005. Coarse-to-fine n-best parsing and maxent discriminative reranking. In *The 43rd Meeting of the Association for Computational Linguistics (ACL)*.

Eugene Charniak. 1997. Statistical parsing with a context-free grammar and word statistics. In *Proceedings of the Fourteenth National Conference on Artificial Intelligence (AAAI)*.

Amit Dubey. 2004. *Statistical Parsing for German: Modeling syntactic properties and annotation differences*. Ph.D. thesis, Saarland University, Germany.

Jennifer Foster, Joachim Wagner, Djamé Seddah, and Josef van Genabith. 2007. Adapting WSJ-trained parsers to the British National Corpus using in-domain self-training. In *Proceedings of the Tenth International Workshop on Parsing Technologies (IWPT)*.

Zhongqiang Huang and Mary Harper. 2009. Self-training pcfg grammars with latent annotations across languages. In *Proceedings of the 2009 Conference on Empirical Methods in Natural Language Processing*, EMNLP '09.

Dan Klein and Chris Manning. 2003. Accurate unlexicalized parsing. In *The 41st Annual Meeting of the Association for Computational Linguistics (ACL)*.

Sandra Kübler. 2005. How do treebank annotation schemes influence parsing results? or how not to compare apples and oranges. In *Proceedings of the 5th International Conference on Recent Advances in Natural Language Processing (RANLP)*.

Sandra Kübler. 2008. The page 2008 shared task on parsing german. In *Proceedings of the ACL Workshop on Parsing German*, Columbus, Ohio.

David McClosky, Eugene Charniak, and Mark Johnson. 2006a. Effective self-training for parsing. In *Human Language Technology conference - North American chapter of the Association for Computational Linguistics annual meeting (HLT-NAACL)*.

David McClosky, Eugene Charniak, and Mark Johnson. 2006b. Reranking and self-training for parser adaptation. In *The 21st International Conference on Computational Linguistics and 44th Annual Meeting of the Association for Computational Linguistics (ACL-COLING)*.

David McClosky, Eugene Charniak, and Mark Johnson. 2008. When is self-training effective for parsing? In *Proceedings of COLING*.

David McClosky, Eugene Charniak, and Mark Johnson. 2010. Automatic domain adaptation for parsing. In *Human Language Technologies: The 2010 Annual Conference of the North American Chapter of the Association for Computational Linguistics*.

Slav Petrov, Leon Barrett, Romain Thibaux, and Dan Klein. 2006. Learning accurate, compact, and interpretable tree annotation. In *The 21st International Conference on Computational Linguistics and 44th Annual Meeting of the Association for Computational Linguistics (ACL-COLING)*.

Ines Rehbein and Josef van Genabith. 2007. Why is it so difficult to compare treebanks? TIGER and TüBa-D/Z revisited. In *Proceedings of the Sixth International Workshop on Treebanks and Linguistic Theories*.

Roi Reichart and Ari Rappoport. 2007. Self-training for enhancement and domain adaptation of statistical parsers trained on small datasets. In *The 45th Annual Meeting of the Association for Computational Linguistics (ACL)*.

Anne Schiller, Simone Teufel, and Christine Thielen. 1995. Guidelines für das Tagging deutscher Textcorpora mit STTS. Technical report, IMS-CL, University Stuttgart, Germany.

Helmut Schmid and Florian Laws. 2008. Estimation of conditional probabilities with decision trees and an application to fine-grained pos tagging. In *Proceedings of the 22nd International Conference on Computational Linguistics*, COLING-08.

Wolfgang Seeker, Ines Rehbein, Jonas Kuhn, and Josef van Genabith. 2010. Hard constraints for grammatical function labelling. In *The 48th Annual Meeting of the Association for Computational Linguistics (ACL)*.

Anders Søgaard. 2011. Data point selection for cross-language adaptation of dependency parsers. In *The 49th Annual Meeting of the Association for Computational Linguistics: Human Language Technologies (ACL-HLT)*.

Mark Steedman, Miles Osborne, Anoop Sarkar, Stephen Clark, Rebecca Hwa, Julia Hockenmaier, Paul Ruhlen, Steven Baker, and Jeremiah Crim. 2003. Bootstrapping statistical parsers from small datasets. In *The 11th Conference of the European Chapter of the Association for Computational Linguistics (EACL)*.

Heike Telljohann, Erhard W. Hinrichs, Sandra Kübler, and Heike Zinsmeister. 2005. Stylebook for the Tübingen Treebank of Written German (TüBa-D/Z). Technical report, University Tübingen, Germany.

Daniel Zeman and Philip Resnik. 2008. Cross-language parser adaptation between related languages. In *Proceedings of IJCNLP 2008 Workshop on NLP for Less Privileged Languages*.

Author Index

Association for Computational Linguistics
209 N. Eighth Street
Stroudsburg, Pennsylvania 18360

CURRAN ASSOCIATES INC
proceedings.com